P9-DUJ-938

DATE DUE

NO 7'99			
MR 30 04			
MR 30 '04			

DEMCO 38-296

A Sacred Journey

A SACRED JOURNEY

The Jewish Quest for a Perfect World

David M. Elcott

JASON ARONSON INC.
Northvale, New Jersey
London

Riverside Community College
APR '97   Library
4800 Magnolia Avenue
Riverside, California 92506

BM 565 .E387 1995

Elcott, David M.

A sacred journey

The author gratefully acknowledges permission to quote from the following sources:

From SURVIVAL IN AUSCHWITZ by Primo Levi, translated by Stuart Woolf; translation copyright © 1959 by The Orion Press, Inc., translation. Original copyright © 1958 by Giulio Einaudi editors S.p.A. Used by permission of Viking Penguin, a division of Penguin Books USA Inc.

From ZOHAR: THE BOOK OF ENLIGHTENMENT, translated by Daniel Chanan Matt. Copyright © 1983 by Daniel Chanan Matt. Used by permission of the publisher, Paulist Press.

This book was set in 12 pt. Berkeley Oldstyle by Alpha Graphics, Pittsfield, New Hampshire.

Copyright © 1995 David M. Elcott

10 9 8 7 6 5 4 3 2 1

All rights reserved. Printed in the United States of America. No part of this book may be used or reproduced in any manner whatsoever without written permission from Jason Aronson Inc. except in the case of brief quotations in reviews for inclusion in a magazine, newspaper, or broadcast.

Library of Congress Cataloging-in-Publication Data

Elcott, David M.
    A sacred journey: the Jewish quest for a perfect world / by David M. Elcott.
      p. cm.
    Includes bibliographical references and index.
    ISBN 1-56821-386-7
    1. Judaism—Essence, genius, nature. 2. Perfection—Religious
aspects—Judaism. 3. Judaism and social problems. 4. Spiritual
life—Judaism. I. Title.
    BM565.E387   1995
    296—dc20   94-43471

Manufactured in the United States of America. Jason Aronson Inc. offers books and cassettes. For information and catalog write to Jason Aronson Inc., 230 Livingston Street, Northvale, New Jersey 07647.

To Mutti, who gave me stories to tell,

and

Talia, Noam, Yaron, and Liore, the best reasons to tell them

CONTENTS

Introduction:

THE TALE OF THE STORYTELLER

I am a bearer and teller of other people's stories. That is not to deny that I have my own story, but it is as yet incomplete and wonderfully dependent on so many others. Like all storytellers, I make no attempt at an impartial reading. In spite of being fully immersed in American life at the end of the twentieth century, the sources out of which I weave my story seem powerfully filtered through the traditions and experiences of the Jewish people. At the same time, I must translate the stories that have come down to me from the past into the language of my own world. This is less presumptuous than it sounds. Jewish tradition relates that every Jew stood at Mount Sinai and received the Torah, yet the sounds resonated differently for each listener. This story, then, is but one refraction of the Torah's message, one storyteller's rendering of a unique people's search for meaning.

To be sure, the Jewish people has inherited many stories, told and retold through the ages. Such stories are vital for a living culture. Each people records its past in sacred texts and in song, through liturgy and dance, art and literature.

Reenactments of ancient legends, calendar celebrations, and the marking of life-cycle events serve to explain and preserve the customs and traditions of a community while nurturing its unique identity. As generations pass, the ancient tales are embellished and molded into language that allows the past to emerge anew to those living centuries later and in radically different circumstances. Jews have carried their stories with them, not only through time but also to every corner of the globe, shaping and reshaping their legacy along the way. This book, then, is a new retelling of the Jewish story, a narrative that spans millennia. It is not a theology nor does it attempt to provide the definitive study of Jewish history. The goal is not to establish a set of principles or locate the true Judaism. My hope is that this book will provide one voice that will speak with excitement and empathy to a reader struggling to adapt familiar stories to new situations.

Specifically, the story told here focuses on the question of meaning: Can the Jewish story provide meaning to human beings living in North America at the end of the twentieth century? The Western civilization in which we participate elevates the individual more than any other society in human history. Our lives here are animated by unprecedented freedoms, power, and affluence. We are told: you must be all that you can be, fulfill your potential and every fantasy as well. Everything can be changed—from hair color to sex, from nationality and religion to career and spouse. The word *impossible* is not part of our vocabulary. The great achievements of science and technology define our world. We can go more places faster and more efficiently. We can track galaxies in the process of formation. We can heal illnesses that once killed millions and operate on a human body with microscopic precision. Today, an individual is likely to have three times the life span of the average Roman and almost twice that of a seventeenth-century European. Yet the search for purpose in life remains particularly elusive for the individual living in our times.

In a world in which new means better, many people have responded by discarding the traditions, values, and institutions inherited from parents and grandparents. How can the traditions that gave meaning to *their* lives be relevant to our own? The consequence of living in an age of rapid change, it often seems, is to exist like an amnesiac without any viable connection to the past. Orphaned from history, we are easily able to satisfy our needs and desires but find it more difficult to experience our own lives as worthwhile. Harold Kushner identifies this malaise:

> I was reading Carl Jung's book *Modern Man in Search of a Soul* one day, when I came across several passages which startled me with their insight. They gave me the feeling that a man who lived before I was born knew me better than I knew myself. The first passage was, "About a third of my cases are suffering from no clinically definable neurosis, but from the senselessness and emptiness of their lives. This can be described as the general neurosis of our time."
>
> I had to admit he was right. . . . What frustrates us and robs our lives of joy is this absence of meaning. Our lives go on day after day. They may be successful or unsuccessful, full of pleasure or full of worry. But do they mean anything?[1]

This deep sense of anomie is all too understandable. After all, why should we experience our existence as meaningful? We are born, we live our lives, however many the years, and then we die, knowing that the constituent chemical and organic parts of our bodies ultimately will be absorbed back into the earth. Even in religious language, one detects a struggle to come to terms with human finitude. In the words of the Jewish High Holiday liturgist:

> Our origin is dust and we return to dust.
> We obtain bread by the peril of our lives
> We are like a fragile potsherd
> Like the grass that withers
> The flower that fades
> The fleeting shadow
> A passing cloud
> Like the wind that blows
> And the dream that vanishes.

Those words are a reminder, even through the poetry of prayer, that life can be viewed as fleeting and without purpose—even in a world imbued with meaning by an unshakable faith in God's presence. In this century, that awareness of obliteration has mutated into a dark terror that haunts the nightmares of all people. Despite the remarkable advances in technology, human life has been devalued in this age as never before. The modern efficiency of genocide has allowed for the wholesale destruction of entire civilizations and the murder of tens of millions of innocents in every corner of the earth.

Possessing this keen awareness of the nature of our universe, it is all too easy to feel an abiding sense of loneliness, of existential emptiness, and from there to slip into the iron grip of despair. It is to counteract this panic that the traditions of Judaism assert: Remember. "Blessed are You, God, who *remembers* the covenant that binds us."[2]

To remember is to stake a claim for purposefulness. To remember is to state: I am worthy of memory. A life is worthy of memory. Life is not one continuous circle, returning on itself over and over again. This story, my story, is worth telling.

Of course, we are more than individuals looking for personal fulfillment. Each of us also is a member of a family, of one or more communities, as well as a partner in the entire human enterprise. So the search for meaning must be social as well, requiring that we find a place and a purpose in relation to others and to the earth on which we live. Judaism approaches the individual's connection to and responsibility toward the larger world in this age by its central belief in *tikkun olam*, the quest for a perfect world. *Tikkun olam* is the force that moves both the individual and the Jewish people forward. The world needs healing to be repaired. Human beings, Jewish tradition asserts, are created in the divine image, partners in completing an unfinished creation.

For many centuries, Jews relied on inherited texts and traditions to provide the meaning that sustained them in viable communities under difficult conditions. At the same time, they were bolstered by their view of the gentile world as alien and evil, a source of spiritual and physical pollution. But if Jews today are to take responsibility for their own lives and for building a better world, they will need to utilize *all* the tools available. The physical and social sciences provide remarkable instruments by which to examine, analyze, and anticipate both the challenges modernity poses and Judaism's potential to provide models by which we can live meaningful lives in this era. Therefore, in addition to utilizing the texts and traditions of Judaism to understand one's role as an architect of change in the world at large, I also intend to use the insights of sociology, psychology, and other academic disciplines to understand the messages of Judaism. To effectively choose one's path today means to be an analyst as well as a practitioner of life. This insight informs the entire book.

I begin, as must all human beings, with personal history. I trace my family through my mother to Germany, although her family retained the memory of arriving in the Rhineland as refugees from Spain. The earliest stories told to me were those of my grandmother, a literate and confirmed "free-thinker," whose family had rejected many of the rituals of Judaism in favor of scientific truths well over a century earlier. But Mutti's stories of our family's experiences in Germany belied her faith in those scientific truths, for her life was filled with a search for transcendence. She found that meaning through her vigorous intellect, while at the same time instilling in her children, grandchildren, and great-grandchildren an awareness of themselves as Jews and as loved human beings created in God's image.

Chapter 1 takes a conscious look at that which Mutti instinctively believed and taught. It presents the Jewish pre-history, which posits a world created with purpose and design, one in which human beings are so significant that they are called nothing less than the image of God. The story of the Jewish people begins precisely with this remarkable idea.

From an idea grows purpose. And here too I find a parallel between the connections of early childhood to active adult life and Judaism's own development from idea to history. My parents fled their childhood homes. My mother left Germany for the United States, determined to keep her past alive and to find meaning in the destruction of her world. She passed that quest on to me. My father escaped from New York City's Harlem to Greenwich Village, then to the Army, and from there to Los Angeles. As the child of immigrants, his burning desire was to realize the American dream. He devoured whatever learning was available to him and transmitted his passion for knowledge to me. My boyhood home, filled with storytelling and love, remains a rich reservoir from which I draw on my sense of the intrinsic purposefulness of life.

On some level, we all know that our assumptions and beliefs are deeply autobiographical, nurtured by personal histories from infancy and childhood deep into adult life. Judaism too makes manifest its formative principles through its unfolding history, never as pure belief disassociated from the past. Indeed, the test of Judaism's validity does not lie in any abstract debate about authority or theology, but rather in how it has played out, generation by generation, in the real lives of real people and in the communities they sustained. Judaism claims a covenant with God, a bilateral responsibility to continuously repair the world and make it more perfect. But a manifesto for future perfection, in and of itself, offers no solace for suffering or pain. In a world in which religious allegiance is mostly voluntary, such a dream will not be compelling enough for one to continue living by Jewish prescripts. Jewish theology insists that embracing its approach will improve the quality of life of its adherents now, in this world. That is the test of Judaism for each individual. And, because Judaism must thrive in this world, history becomes the testing ground for its broader assumptions: Are the conditions of life improving? Has Judaism and have Jews contributed to positive transformations in world history? Can human beings look to the future with hope?

In fact, the Jewish vision of perfecting the world already has shaped humanity through its offshoots of Christianity, Islam, and Western culture, yet the work is by no means done. Chapters 2 through 7 retell the story of Judaism through the lens of its history: the revolutionary struggles of the Jewish people to transform the world by seeking fundamental changes in the social, political, and economic circumstances of Jews and all human beings. The retelling of the challenges facing Abraham and Sarah, the dramas of the Exodus and Sinai along with wanderings in deserts and diasporas, the religious quests of poet kings, rabbis, and mystics provide the intellectual and spiritual data needed to interpret and engage the consistent themes of Judaism in our own time.

Out of history, we arrive at the present, with its challenge of how to live our lives in the fullest possible way. I matured in twin worlds, a child of the turbulent sixties and a participant in the experiments to rebuild the Jewish people both in Israel and in the United States. This led me to a doctorate at Columbia University in political psychology and Middle East studies, to study and work in Israel, and to my commitment to Jewish renewal through education.

My professional life continued my education. I had the privilege of a nine-year spiritual and intellectual internship with Harold Schulweis and a ten-year term (and continuing) with Irving (Yitz) Greenberg. Both men are visionaries who allowed me to reimagine what Judaism could be. Both men are revolutionaries who overturn complacency wherever they go. Both these teachers propound a Judaism imbued with a distinctly Jewish method for seeking the sacred through the discipline of commitments, voluntarily chosen. From Harold Schulweis I learned:

> To find the world interesting lies at the heart of Judaism. To be a Jew of faith is to be anything but bored. To be a Jew is not to yawn away one's life, but to stand slack-jawed in amazement at the world of possibilities and to rise with excitement toward its realization.[3]

In particular, Irving Greenberg's insights into the nature of being human nurtured by the realization that we are created in God's image, his interpretations of the implications of covenant and redemption, the impact of the Holocaust on the voluntary nature of the covenant, and his search for uncovering sacredness in secularity have framed chapters of this book even as we await the completion of his own. The words I write are so infused with the wisdom, passion, and insights of this profound thinker and teacher that I could not identify all his contributions. I am honored and grateful simply to be one of his commentators.

How can we move beyond the destruction that fills our newspapers to the dream of paradise? By raising the commonplace to the sacred. Judaism's method of seeking the sacred is through the discipline of voluntary commitments, which offers a mature path to a vibrant Judaism, as well as a unique way of addressing and fully living life. Over three millennia, Jews accepted their covenantal responsibility by nurturing a system of behaviors called *mitzvot*. These *mitzvot* guided them through complex decision-making and allowed Judaism to flourish under the most adverse conditions. Chapter 8 will explore the Jewish methods of seeking sacredness through the acceptance of *mitzvot*.

Every day, Jews committed to their traditions are asked to apply the ideas of Judaism and its *mitzvot* to unfamiliar situations. That is a challenge addressed by the National Jewish Center for Learning and Leadership (CLAL), which analyzes and explores new directions for the North American Jewish community. Through research and shared study in an extraordinary collegial setting, the faculty confronts the multiple challenges of Jewish leadership today. I have been wonderfully challenged by this remarkable group of colleagues who so influence my mind, soul, and heart. In particular, I have been guided by the wisdom of Reuven Kimelman and the sharp intelligence and critiques tempered with patient encouragement of my colleagues David Kraemer and Irwin Kula. My debt to Steve Greenberg, David Nelson, Tsvi Blanchard and all my colleagues at CLAL and to the friends who have supported the Center's growth is beyond measure; their voices and insights are found throughout this text.

What I have acquired through our shared study and dialogues is an understanding that we who live today can rely exclusively neither on the vision of a distant future nor on the past versions of the Jewish story to guide contemporary decision-making. Valuable as the past may be, its application to a next generation has always been problematic. Moderns have questioned the inherent value of the past, seeing change itself as a fundamental good. Rapid change *is* a central feature of our lives, but the direction and success of any particular change is often determined by how the past is understood and how its lessons are implemented. The task of each generation of Jews has been to confront life by linking the Jewish story with Judaism's unique method of seeking sacredness through *mitzvot*. Chapter 9 demonstrates how the task may be accomplished by applying the insights and methodologies of Judaism to real-life, contemporary situations. It illustrates Judaism's fundamental approach, which asks one not simply to dream, but instead to patiently implement a vision of repairing the world. This chapter on *tzedakah*— applied social justice—offers a uniquely Jewish approach to healing suffering in the world.

Life is lived in its particulars; theology for me is less speculation than the product of intimacies with other human beings. I married with great self-assurance and a bagful of truths. Yet in my discovery of another person, I encountered new worlds, new emotions, new thoughts—as well as new uncertainties. In diving into love with Shira, I was chastened into modesty about the truths I held dear and liberated by insights that grew out of our relationship. I became a better teacher, because I was more open to the complexity of the world, as well as a more whole and loving human being. Chapter 10 is informed by the challenge and excitement of facing the unknown. Judaism's fearlessness in confronting the future allows its followers to celebrate the creative possibilities of indeterminacy, of constructing a family and community without demanding absolute truths to guide them. It confirms that interaction with the universe we inhabit will continue to unfold, illumined by new insights, heightened human capacities, and unpredictable alterative courses of action. Shira helped me see Judaism and my own life this way, allowing me to recognize my own frailties and moments of confusion and weakness, yet view these moments as new possibilities for understanding and decision-making. Through her, I have learned that Judaism nurtures the dissonances that fill the human heart and mind, for these dissonances can be united in God's oneness. My life and my being are graced through her.

I have traveled throughout North America and Israel collecting in my bag the fantasies, pains, anxieties, and celebrations of countless students, friends, family members, and colleagues who so passionately want their Judaism to be significant in their lives. Much contained in this book belongs to them, the outgrowth of discussions lasting late into the night. It was through their powerful stories that I was able to hear the voices of those who feel too exhausted to be architects of change and too hurt to bear the burden of Jewish commitment to repair the world. They have taught me about healing. And the final chapter of this book, "Healing and Wholeness," returns to the Jewish vision of the world as one that *can* be healed. While many of us live with anxieties, fears, and angers in facing what often seems like the insurmountable task of living, Judaism teaches us that these feelings have been experienced before and that there are remedies for despair. The words of the Torah and of later Jewish texts are full of empathetic voices—a multitude of responses to our own pains and confusions waiting to be appropriated. Jewish traditions all maintain that, as human beings, we are part of something larger than each individual's life span, that we can experience love and that life is intrinsically meaningful. Jewish traditions are reminders that even in those moments when a person feels inadequate and incomplete, he or she can have confidence in the planned order and goodness of the universe, faith that God's presence can be experienced in a life of loving relationships, and hope in the inherent meaningfulness of one's own life. Judaism affirms that we are not alone.

The final chapter of this book brings me back to a beginning. For this work truly began with the births of our four children. Each one proves again that human beings are delightfully unique, filled with limitless potential and an innate Godlike dignity. Not only am I unable to answer my children's questions, but I have learned through them that power and authority, the mainstay of traditional American and Jewish life, must now be replaced by relationship and dialogue. Talia, Noam, Yaron, and Liore have taught me that love is infinite and that life's meanings are found less in lofty doctrines and endless words than in the celebration of shared quests and experiences. My children already have enriched my own story, even as they add to the larger one of the Jewish people and humanity as a whole.

And so, as a storyteller, I return to the stories—mine and others. All must be heard and absorbed, because Judaism today cannot be translated into a singular, universal voice. There are only stories to be told, many times over, each with different images and meanings reflecting the uniqueness of each storyteller and each telling of the story. I am, in particular, grateful that David Behrman, Joseph Telushkin, Jonathan Woocher, Barbara Friedman, and Radine Spier encouraged me to find a way to put into print the torrent of words they patiently endured as I discussed these stories with them. Channeling that torrent, focusing the stories, and clarifying their meaning was a burden assumed with talent by my editor, Sarah Brzowsky. Her patience and skill carried this book into being. And my gratitude goes to Yvonne Grant for her patient retyping.

All of these dramatic and mundane stories, and more, make up my life's story, which is part of the history of a people. For the most part, history tells the grand stories, recalling the actions of the powerful, the wars and conspiracies of monarchs and warriors. Yet real life consists of the smaller, more intimate events and activities we experience and witness. In these are contained the seeds of transcendence. That awareness should cause us to turn our heads and regard, as did Moses, the Burning Bush.

Moses walked over to examine the commonplace and found it exceptional. He looked more closely at the natural and discovered in it the supernatural.

Can you imagine this, he must have said. I climb a mountain looking for a lamb and look what I find? You see, there was this regular, old bush—everybody else kept strolling along, but I was intrigued. And a Voice. It told me about the past, about a promise to be kept, and I decided to listen. I found sacredness in a thornbush and meaning in my struggles.

Moses looked, found it *kadosh*—sacred—and recorded the memory. Jews call that record Torah. And each generation of Jews adds to Torah by retelling the story and giving it meaning again. Little did Moses know that in that act of re-examining the commonplace he began a rebellion whose echoes still motivate seekers of freedom millennia later.

As David Roskies notes, to sustain memory, record history, and give it meaning is an aggressively affirmative act.[4] In their passion to record the past and make it live, Jews are an aggressively affirmative people. To read the ancient texts, to sing the songs and chant the venerated words, to struggle to re-tell in the language of today the story of a people over three thousand years old, is to stop before multiple bushes aflame with potential and to elevate all the common moments of life to the sacred. In so doing, a people authors the memories which will compose the Torah of its age.

1

IN THE IMAGE OF GOD

We do not know why the universe came into being exactly when it did, just as we do not know why one particular egg and sperm combine to become a particular full-size human being. That is not to say that we do not have an abundance of data about the formation of the universe or the conception of a baby—only that when we add up all the facts, we still don't know toward what end these births occurred.

Even so, the Jewish people has cherished a tradition that human life has a purpose, which begins outside the natural realm. Whether this belief can be scientifically verified is not the issue here. Rather, we are examining how this basic belief helped the Jewish people to make sense out of their lives as well as to seek to improve the quality of human existence. It is the foundation upon which the Jewish people has narrated its own history.

THE ROLE OF TORAH

The Jewish narrative begins with Torah. Torah is not simply the five books of Moses that comprise the first part of the

1

Jewish Bible. Torah is the blueprint for the Jewish understanding of the world. The word *Torah* expands in Jewish tradition to encompass all that is important in life. It means "the teaching" par excellence, or the source of "light," or "enlightenment." The meaning of Torah goes beyond specific words or interpretations. The *Zohar*, a central text of the mystical kabbalists that was written by Moses de Leon at the end of the thirteenth century, tries to capture its ineffable meaning through metaphor:

In descending to this world,
if the Torah did not put on the garments of this world
the world could not endure.
So this story of Torah (the Five Books of Moses) is but the garment
  of Torah.

The body is clothed in garments,
the stories of this world.
Fools of the world look only at the garment,
the story of Torah; they know nothing more.
Those who know more do not look at the garment
but rather at the body under that garment. . . .
In the time to come they are destined to look at the soul of the
  soul of Torah.

As wine must sit in a jar,
so Torah must sit in a garment.
Look only at what is under the garment!
So all those words and all those stories—
they are [mere] garments!

Happy are the righteous who look at Torah properly.[1]

There are many ways to read the Torah. Some people read the words of the Torah with complete faith, believers in the infallibility of the divine word. Others see God's hand in the way the Bible was transmitted from one generation to another. There also are those who find literary beauty or moral power in what they consider to be a very human text. In addition, for many Jews, Christians, and Muslims, reading the words of the Bible has a profound personal meaning. The Torah also can be read analytically, in order to explore the cultural heritage of a particular people. Faith is not a prerequisite for this study, only a reader who is able to be conscious of the many levels of text and who constantly asks why the story is told as it is.

The Torah provides a method by which to understand the human condition. By questioning the particular slant of its stories, by probing words used and unused, a person searching for truths can find answers to the perennial questions that have plagued humankind: "So what? What difference does anything make?" Here, for example, is how the language of the Torah's opening words suggest one answer to the questions of meaning:

> When God set about to create the heavens and the earth, the earth being unformed and void, with darkness hovering over the face of the depths and a divine wind sweeping over the waters, God said, "Let there be light," and there was light. God saw that the light was good, and God divided the light from the darkness. God called the light day, and the darkness God called night. And there was evening and there was morning; the first day. . . . God said, "Let there be lights in the breadth of the heavens to separate day from night, signs for the set times, days and years. . . ." And it was so. . . . And God saw that it was good. . . .
> And God said, "Let us make a human in the divine image, after the divine likeness. They shall rule the fish of the

oceans, the birds in the sky, the large animals, the whole
earth, and all forms of life that creep on earth." And God
created a human in the divine image, in the image of the
Divine God created it; male and female, God created them.
(Genesis 1:1-6, 24-26)

The first chapter of Genesis clearly is neither a chronol-
ogy of events nor a scientific explanation of how the world
came into being. Rather, its description of creation comes to
answer the question of *meaning*. To one who argues that life
is a series of random flukes and coincidences, the Torah
proclaims that the world was created with intent and design,
that stars shine, seasons change, planets rotate according to
plan. To one who fears that the universe is spinning chaoti-
cally toward a black hole, the Torah repeats that, at each step
of the way, God saw (and sees) creation and life as good.
This narrative that formed the Jewish people describes a
universe progressing from chaos to order and from lifelessness to even more life. To one who suspects that life has no
intrinsic value, the opening verses of Genesis describe how
each person was created in God's image. A tradition that
asserts that each human being is born with a touch of Godliness cannot help but affect how a person feels about himself or herself—even that person who questions God's existence. To highlight this point, the *Mishnah* offers the following
commentary:

Rabbi Akiva said: How greatly God must have loved us to
create us in the Divine image; yet even greater love did God
show us in raising our consciousness to know that we are
created in the Divine image.[2]

But the consciousness of the divine within has implications—and raises new questions. For how do men and women imbued with an eternal divine spark affirm life against the painful awareness of human evil, frailty, and mortality? To speak the language of a humanity in God's image cannot simply be sweetness or metaphor. It must stand as a principle even as it is assaulted by an ambiguous reality. Human beings may well damage one another, friends do suffer painful and prolonged deaths even as I must confront my own mortality. Yet, in spite of this evidence to the contrary, the natural world yields rich proofs that all of life is not doomed to inevitable death and decay. Looking beyond any one death to the evolution of life and life-forms, a very different conclusion can be reached. In the battle of life against death, life is winning.

I am indebted to Irving Greenberg for the central insights that I used as the basis for my exploration of the opening passage of the Torah. Specifically, Greenberg teaches that the first chapter of Genesis challenges us to see that reality is not exhausted by a surface reading but, rather, there are three decisive movements underlying existence: the movement from chaos to order, from nonlife to life, and from less complex forms of life to life more and more like God. Judaism calls the highest form human, an image of God. All of life moves in this direction and the human challenge is to become part of the rhythm of these movements until there is nothing less than what Greenberg labels a Triumph of Life.

The Jewish story from Genesis emphasizes that, previous to God's conscious act of creation, there was no life, only chaotic matter, "void and unformed." The pattern of creation after God's first words is incremental. Life evolves day by day.

The Torah provides no explanation for all this, other than to indicate God's will expressed as, "Let there be . . ." The movement from nonlife to life remains a mystery, but the unfolding process is declared a product of God's will.

Science has postulated that at that very early point in the story of the world, life was overwhelmed by nonlife, by senseless matter, crashing meteorites and swirling toxic gases. Hundreds of millions of years later, the earth could barely sustain the initial protocells that would herald a transformation on this planet. Yet inexorably, life-forms multiplied and diversified, reforming in new, more intricate combinations. As these life-forms became more sophisticated in their capacity to reproduce—moving from asexual to sexual reproduction—even greater diversity emerged.

Initially, the earth was an arid mass. The first drops of water were devoid of life. It took many aeons to produce a drop of pond water exploding with life. That explosion spread throughout the water bodies of the earth, into streams and rivers, ocean waves and the chemically complex cauldrons of the deep sea. More extraordinary still, new life-forms then began to emerge from the water to inhabit the land, which was soon crawling with ever more abundant and complex life. Yet all these life-forms derived from the same source:

> But it seems very clear that there's only one hereditary line leading to all life now on Earth. Every organism is a relative, a distant cousin, of every other. This is manifest when we compare how all the organisms on Earth do business, how they're built, what they're made of, what genetic language they speak, and especially how similar their blueprints and molecular job orders are. All life is kin.[3]

The idea that the DNA of human beings as well as the DNA of all living organisms can be traced back to a single-cell life-form is powerful testimony to the relentless growth of life against lifelessness—life that is ever expanding, changing, reproducing, recombining, and filling more and more of the universe.

It is not only the quantity of life which has increased. The more remarkable insight is that life, in its drive to complexity, also becomes more and more like God. From the Jewish perspective, a single cell—while miraculous—is a more rudimentary and primitive image of God than a reptile, which in turn is less like God than a mammal that nurtures life in its womb and feeds its young. Chimpanzees, whose active DNA structure is more than 98 percent identical to that of human beings, are less in the image of God than are people. As human beings develop and extend their capacities, utilizing more of their intelligence, they display features more akin to God. Human beings, who remember stories, experience emotions, think consciously, and have the capacity of self-reflection, inch ever closer to the ideal divine image. At this juncture, human beings appear to be the most like God, but experience indicates that life will continue to evolve.

God represents life and the power of life against all that is "void and unformed." The opening chapters of the Torah do not deal with wars over territory or conflicts between kings but with a far more significant battle: the battle against chaos and death. The forces of chaos, those tendencies in the universe that spin away from order, are an ever-present threat to the universe. In the poetry of the psalmist, God battles to hold back the chaos, so that life can be protected and flourish:

It was You who drove back the sea with Your might,
who smashed the heads of the monsters in the waters . . .
it was You who released springs and torrents,
who made mighty rivers run dry;
the day is Yours, the nights also;
it was You who set in place the globe of the sun;
You fixed all the boundaries of the earth;
summer and winter—You made them. (Psalms 74:12-17)

Jews see their essential challenge embedded in the opening text of their story: Their role as human beings is to become the allies of God, engaging like God in a battle against chaos and death, aware that the potential for disorder is ever present.[4]

Life is defeating death in yet another sense. I can look into myself and recognize a replication of cells that I inherited, cells that themselves are replicas of my ancestors. In fact, of course, they are recombined DNA, producing the unique genetic organism that is me. But the fact that every cell in my body is inextricably linked to my past—a past that leads back to the very first human beings, to the earliest moments of life and beyond—also links me to a chain of life of which I am but the latest (and, from the human vantage point, the most sophisticated) form. With bits of my ancestors surviving in me, all the lives that preceded me have not died. At the same time, as a father of four children, I can experience the triumph of life even as I recognize my own mortality.

This is not to advance some popular notion about the oneness of the universe (although there are truths in that, too), but to emphasize the simple biological fact that the evolution of life depends on cells encoded with their unique genetic messages from the past, as well as on one's willingness and ability to reproduce cells. Over time, dysfunctional mutations are lost while new features, slowly acquired to help sustain life, are replicated. Human DNA chains are replete with patterns no longer operational—instructions for producing tails or fins or gills, for instance—yet their traces remain part of each person:

> These are not only the surviving annals of the history of life, but also handbooks of mechanisms of evolutionary change. The field of molecular evolution—only a few decades old—permits us to decode the record at the heart of life on Earth. Pedigrees are written in these sequences, carrying us back not a few generations, but most of the way to the origin of life. Molecular biologists have learned to read them and calibrate the profound kinship of all life on Earth.[5]

Thus, a newborn baby's ancestry goes back millions of years, to the primal moment when life itself began. The awareness that life has become increasingly complex and diverse must give us confidence about the future: We know that, with everything we have inherited as humans, we can produce a new generation that has even more potential to be born in God's image than those that came before. This resonates with the first claim the Torah makes on humans, that they are to bring more life into the world by continuing to create through their own bodies.

This is the thrust of the narrative in the first chapter of the Torah. One need not agree on the literal meaning of the words or feel obligated to ascertain the authorship of the text in order to allow the story to nourish a sense of life force growing in quantity and complexity each day. Jean-Paul Sartre understands such power:

A man is always a teller of tales, he lives surrounded by his
stories and the stories of others, he sees everything that happens to him through them; and he tries to live his own life
as if he were telling a story.[6]

This affirmative story of a whole people defies the position that life originated in blind luck, that existence is nothing more than a cosmic coincidence, and that consequently
one can depend on nothing else—including the future. Judaism rebels against such nihilism. It sees conscious artistry
and a planned unfolding in the remarkable symbiosis of elements that nurture more and more life.

The rabbis who taught and wrote in the first centuries of
the Common Era were great disciples of the belief that life is
intrinsically valuable and that human beings are its apogee.
They could locate this love of life and commitment to it in
the strangest places, even while debating a death sentence
for a heinous capital crime. Irving Greenberg's insights are
most important here. Greenberg teaches that the orienting
principle of the Jewish way is that every human being is an
image of God. Using the Mishnah as a commentary on image
of God, Greenberg teaches that every human being has three
intrinsic dignities: infinite value, equality, and uniqueness.
These dignities need to be affirmed and realized in the political, economics, and social spheres if we are to increase the
quality of life. In the *Mishnah Sanhedrin*, it is noted that a
witness to a crime such as murder would be cautioned before
his testimony with the following admonition:

Perhaps you are not aware that we shall scrutinize your testimony by serious cross-examination and inquiry? Know that
capital cases are not like monetary cases. In civil cases, one

makes monetary restitution. . . . But in capital cases [the witness] is responsible for the blood of the accused and even of all his descendants to the end of time.[7]

It is not the accused who is interrogated by the judges of the court, but the *witness,* who has the power, through his testimony, to convict the defendant and cause his or her execution. The blood that may be shed is that of the accused, and the witness must bear the full weight of ending another's life. The rabbinic courts were not known for their death sentences. Some rabbis noted that if a court were to put a person to death once every seventy years, it would be deemed a "bloody court." If the judges in a murder case voted unanimously for a death sentence, the judgment was voided, since at least one judge should have sustained a shred of doubt. The rabbis used this discussion to emphasize their passionate commitment to life and human responsibility to increase life in the world. The Mishnah continues:

> For this reason was a single human being created [first], to teach you that whoever destroys a single soul, Scripture condemns that person as though he [or she] had destroyed a complete world; and whoever saves a single soul, Scripture honors that person as though he [or she] has saved a complete world.[8]

Here, the rabbis affirm a Jewish tradition that any human life, even that of a criminal, should be perceived as having infinite value. The evidence of their day, as of ours, could make the opposite point. The market value of slaves had dropped precipitously during the time of the rabbis, as ever more Jews were sold into slavery by the Romans. Today, millions of children die needlessly for want of dehydration pills or antibiotics. In China, prenatal ultrasound tests insure that male babies will live and female fetuses will be aborted. Yet Judaism still imagines that, as the world improves, the value of human life will increase until, like God, it will be infinite.

The Jewish belief is that *all* life must be supported. The Mishnah stresses the equality of all human beings and avoids any claims of Jewish superiority:

> [One human was created at first] for the sake of peace among human beings, that no one could say to another, "My parent was greater than yours."[9]

It is hard to imagine how Jews, defeated and oppressed by different nations over the centuries, avoided the obvious psychological defense of claiming greater ancestry. That is not to say that the rabbis did not feel a moral superiority to the pagan nations, including Rome, that had conquered them. But they rejected the idea of natural distinctions between human beings, seeing God as a loving and nurturing parent to each and every person. The claim of the nascent American republic that "all men are created equal" (excluding non-Caucasians and women) finds its roots in the Torah's insight that, if only one human being were created by God, we must therefore be related by virtue of sharing the same ancestor. The vision of all people born of a single human being who was fashioned in the image of God, of course, contradicts the ample evidence around us of hierarchies, homelessness, and class divisions. But Judaism insists that the failure of the principle of equality lies not in divine will but in human corruption.

The same Mishnah ends with a point that elevates the human being ever higher by stressing that each individual is unique:

> Again, to claim the greatness of the Holy One, blessed be God: If a person mints many coins from one mold, they all resemble each other, but [God] fashioned every human being in the stamp of the first human, yet not one person is identical to another. Therefore, every single person is obligated to say: "The world was created for my sake."[10]

The rabbis have staked a claim about the way the world ought to be: Each human being, regardless of birth, status, or native ability, has the right to be seen as created as an image of God, filled with infinite worth, equal to all other human beings, and so unique that he or she can say that the world exists only for them. On the other hand, since each and every person can make these claims, the only way all people can create a world that recognizes them is through relationship, that is, the partnership between each person and God, as well as the connections between all human beings. The traditions of Judaism, which build on this fundamental philosophy, provide mechanisms by which such a world can be achieved.

The most profound example of the Jewish will to sustain, nourish, and promote life over death is the rabbinic decree that all the laws of Judaism save three may be ignored and even transgressed if such action may save a life. Joseph B. Soloveitchik, the dean of American Orthodoxy, told the story of his grandfather who, upon turning on a light in the room of a sick person on the Sabbath, was chastised by a fellow Jew for his transgression with the admonition, "But Rabbi, I thought that you are very stringent in your observance of the

Sabbath." The rabbi responded, "But I am even more stringent in my obligation to sustain life."

As Irwin Kula explains:

> Human life is a narrative enterprise. We live surrounded
> by our stories and the stories of others and we see every-
> thing that happens to us through them. As a people, we
> have a rich heritage of stories that we tell—stories that were
> formative in our emergence as a civilization and that con-
> tinue to distinguish us, motivate behavior, inspire us and
> generate a sense of belonging and continuity. These cen-
> tral narratives are the cultural DNA that govern the way
> we see reality and the way we behave. They profoundly
> shape us; and as much as we may author our stories, our
> stories have authority over us.[11]

The Rabbis, of course, knew nothing of genetic theories,
DNA replication, and the common biological ancestry of all
human beings. The idea that each person is so valuable that
he or she is described as being created in the divine image
was a belief, not a scientific theory. The belief has ramifications that the scientific theory does not; for despite what we
know of the evolution of life, no study of biology will conclude that all human beings are of infinite worth, born with
inherent equality, and possessing unquestionable uniqueness. And no scientist can state confidently that life will increase and fill up more and more of the world until it con-
quers death. Those are beliefs that spring from a conviction
that the story that nurtured the Jewish people is still true.
From this seed, that God created the world in love, Judaism
emerged and flourished, taking on the quest for a perfect
world.

2

BUILDING A COVENANT:
AN EVOLVING RELATIONSHIP

What is fascinating to explore in the poetry of the creation epic is not whether it depicts a scientifically accurate version of how this world came into being, but rather what, as a formative Jewish text, it has to say about human beings and the nature of existence. In the traditions set forth, human beings are given mastery over the animal and physical world. They also possess a will that is independent of God. The rabbis articulated this well when they coined the phrase: "All is in the hands of God except for awe [fear] of God."[1] Since, for the sages of the Talmud, awe of God would determine one's behavior, the freedom to believe or not believe in God constitutes the source of human independence.

And as humans are, unlike other forms of life, uniquely independent, this characteristic allows them to establish a relationship with God that is different from that of any other creature in the universe. A powerful Jewish tradition states that human beings are *shutafei Hakadosh Barukh Hu*, partners with God. This partnership, which is first inferred in the

story of the creation, becomes another pillar in the foundation of Judaism. It is as partners in a covenant, or *brit,* with
God, that Jews understand their role in completing God's
initial acts of creation. Judaism has the audacity to declare
that God and humans must respond to each other from
within their relationship. Michael Wyschograd writes:

> To believe in God is to have a psychological relationship with
> God. . . . It includes some negative feelings: anger, jealousy,
> fear, envy, etc. As we open ourselves to others, they gain
> power over us, and this is never without pain and therefore
> hostility. To live with another is to become vulnerable to him
> and therefore to want to protect oneself . . . to know his
> orientation, what he strives for, what matters and what does
> not.[2]

This covenant between God and humanity initially defines
and demands a relationship but not yet specific tasks, roles,
or terms. One could argue that Jewish history is the experience of a people's evolution and transformation in its relationship with God.

Had the world been created perfect, there would be no
need for partnership and no role for a covenant. If humans
were not conscious of the lack of perfection in the world,
they could not be partners. The more conscious people are
of the world around them and their roles within it, the better partners they can be.

At one time, it was assumed that many infants and mothers would die at childbirth, that slavery was normal, and that
pain is natural. Indeed, many around the world continue to
accept these facts as unchanging realities. Such acceptance
of extreme suffering is a reminder that, in the beginning,
human beings were novices at the task of repairing the world.

The partnership was not equal; the human role was over-whelmingly junior. People understood their role as recognizing and praising God's power to hold back the forces of chaos. That is the dynamic expressed in the voice of God speaking out of the whirlwind to Job:

Where were you when I laid the earth's foundations?
Who set its cornerstone
When the morning stars sang together,
Who closed the seas behind doors
When it gathered forth out of the womb?
Have you ever commanded the day to break,
Assigned the dawn its place? (Excerpts from Job, chapter 38)

Human beings accepted God's will and trained themselves to be humble and obedient servants of God. Today, many point to such attitudes as proof that the cost of religious belief is passivity in the face of evil or pain, and that an acceptance of God's will saps human initiative. Judaism struggles with the tensions of a faith that, on the one hand, demands obedience to God and, on the other hand, declares that human beings are active and powerful partners with God. This tension exemplifies but one of Judaism's dialectics: obedience and rebellion, acceptance and protest coexist within Jewish traditions. Faith, unlike logic, resonates honestly to the dissonances that live within the human psyche; the tensions remain.

The saga that unfolds in the early part of the Torah reveals God's tensions as the original divine plan went somewhat awry. Having been granted enormous power and independent will, human beings, inevitably perhaps, extend beyond the limits that God has established, even imagining that they themselves are gods. They reject obedience to God and question the very nature of their role as partner. At the same time, God has difficulty adjusting to the presence of independent human beings in the universe. Exasperated and angry at Adam and Eve's defiance, God strikes out by cursing them with pain and eviction. God condemns the very qualities that had defined human beings created in God's own image:

> Now that the human beings have become like one of us, knowing good and bad, what if they should stretch out their hand and take also from the tree of life, and live forever? (Genesis 3:22)

And so the first partners of God, humans created from dust and the breath of God in God's own image, are banished forever from the Garden of Eden and from their state of perfect relationship with God.

The story continues. God and human beings grow increasingly frustrated as the world repeatedly is damaged by human destructiveness and divine retribution. Cain murders his brother, Abel, and we are told that Cain's descendants continue the violence. The Torah, in the hyperbolic language of disappointment, chastises human beings for diminishing human dignity. Viewing the murder of Abel by his brother Cain, God seems to cry in pain and disbelief:

> What have you done? Listen, your brother's blood cries out to Me from the ground. Therefore, you shall be more cursed than the ground which opened its mouth to receive your brother's blood from your hand. As you work the soil, it will cease to yield its strength to you. You shall wander forever across the earth. (Genesis 4:10-12)

The essential qualities of creation—life, equality, infinite value, uniqueness, goodness, and light—are negated through human acts of murder, enslavement, and abuse of the environment.

Eventually, God inundates the world with a violent flood that ends the original creation, save for one family, the clan of Noah:

> The Lord saw how great was human's wickedness on earth, and how every plan devised by the human's mind was nothing but evil all the time. And the Lord regretted making humans on earth, and God's heart was saddened. The Lord said, "I will blot out from the earth human beings whom I created—together with beasts, creeping things, and birds of the sky; for I regret that I made them." (Excerpts from Genesis, chapter 6)

When the land dries, and Noah the hero offers a sacrifice in praise of God, the divine response informs us that the partnership with all humanity to perfect the world no longer exists:

> The Lord smelled the pleasing aroma, and the Lord thought: Never again will I doom the earth because of humanity, since the devisings of the human mind are evil from youth. (Genesis 8:21)

The lofty idea of a partnership between God and all human beings initially failed. Jewish tradition relates that human beings were much happier turning away from their roles as *shutafei Hakadosh Barukh Hu*, partners of a covenant. After the Flood, the Torah abandons its hopes for all humanity, and focuses on a single couple, Abraham and Sarah. Their trek from the Tigris-Euphrates Valley to *Eretz Yisrael*, the Land of Israel, initiates a continuous encounter between their heirs and God:

> The Lord said to Abram: "Go forth from your native land and from your father's home to the land that I will show you.
> I will make of you a great nation,
> And I will bless you;
> I will make your name great
> And you shall be a blessing.
> I will bless those that bless you
> And curse him that curses you;
> And all the families of the earth
> Shall bless themselves by you."
>
> Abram went forth as the Lord had commanded him. And they set out for the land of Canaan. And the Lord said, "I will assign this land to your offspring." (Genesis 12:1-10, excerpts)

In the story of this journey, one already sees the outlines of the challenges their descendants will face in their own land and in relation to other nations. The lives and struggles of Abraham and Sarah create the paradigm from which meaning will be extracted in the lives of their progeny.

From these verses, Jews remind themselves that Sarah and Abraham's descendants were promised fame, fortune, wealth, power, and land, and that their children and children's children would be eternally protected. Jews were taught to believe not only that they would be "a great people" in their own land but also that they would influence the rest of the world as "a blessing." These somewhat overwhelming promises are the initial source of the concept of Jewish chosenness—as well as the flip side of that idea, the separation of Jews from the rest of humanity. For Jews, the result of this early imprinting is a sense of purposeful superiority alongside painful isolation. It is a complicated legacy. First the Torah exults that all humans are created in God's image and then it isolates two individuals whose heirs are promised a distinct relationship with God, a renewed covenant for which they will serve as witness of God's justice and righteousness. A heightened belief in the value of Jews and the denigration and envy of non-Jews are all part of the Jewish psyche. The tension of Jewish relations with other peoples has resulted in hostility and great suffering, as well as the persistence of the idea of Jewish uniqueness and the desire to repair the world to benefit all human beings. Once again, the dialectic tensions remain unresolved.

Out of the initial encounter between God and Abraham, when God directs him to leave his home and travel to *Eretz Yisrael*, a complex and challenging relationship grows. Neither Abraham nor Sarah are simply obedient. God promises them a child but fails to deliver, and Abraham takes God to task. When Abraham finally is told that his postmenopausal wife will bear the child, this model of a faithful Jew throws himself on his face and laughs at God.

Can a child be born to a man one hundred years old,
Or can Sarah bear a child at ninety? (Genesis 17:17)

And when informed that the wicked inhabitants of Sodom and Gomorrah are to be destroyed, Abraham chastises God and questions God's commitment to divine justice.

Will You sweep away the innocent with the guilty . . . ? Far
be it from You to do such a thing, to bring death upon the
innocent as well as the guilty, so that the innocent and guilty
fare alike. Far be it from You! Shall not the Judge of all the
earth deal justly? (Genesis 18:23-25)

Abraham even tries to dissuade Sarah when she demands
that Abraham's other son, Ishmael, be sent away so that Isaac
can inherit what was promised to him by God. Sarah fights
to protect her only child. Attuned to the implications behind
the story, one cannot help but be struck by characters who
bargain with God and a God who expects Abraham and Sarah
to put up a fight.

Only when God commands Abraham to sacrifice his be-
loved son does the progenitor of the Jewish people become
mute:

> Some time afterward, God put Abraham to the test. God said
> to him, "Abraham," and he answered, "Here I am." And God
> said, "Take your son, your favored one, Isaac, whom you love,
> and go to the land of Moriah, and offer him there as a burnt
> offering on one of the heights that I will point out to you."
> So early next morning, Abraham saddled his ass and took
> with him two of his servants and his son Isaac. He split the
> wood for the burnt offering, and he set out for the place of
> which God had told him. (Genesis 21:1-5)

For so many years, Abraham has basked in divine blessings
of property and children and intimacy with God. Now, he
is asked to do the impossible. If Abraham refuses, he saves
Isaac but loses the covenantal partnership with God. If he
murders Isaac, the proof that the covenant is real will die.
Either choice must throw Abraham into a chasm of insan-

ity. Why does Abraham not waver? Why does he not lose his mind?

Abraham has spent a lifetime struggling in his relationship with God. Abraham experimented with God, slowly developing trust, more even than faith, allowing love to emerge as the product of his relationship with the divine. After a lifetime, Abraham was not obedient, but committed—bound to a covenantal relationship. He realized that faith in the hard-won relationship with God must coexist with his own existential rational and reasonable judgment. Or, rather, there is no judgment that does not include faith as the crucial component of making a decision. Abraham took Isaac to the mountain and prepared to sacrifice him. Had he chosen otherwise, he would not even have been a footnote in history and the Jewish people would not be here.

> The angel of the Lord called to Abraham a second time from heaven, and said, "By Myself I swear, the Lord declares: Because you have done this and have not withheld your son, your favored one, I will bestow My blessing upon you and make your descendants as numerous as the stars of heaven and the sands on the seashore; and your descendants shall seize the gates of their foes. All the nations of the earth shall bless themselves by your descendants, because you have obeyed My command." (Genesis 22:15-18)

One cannot learn from the life of Abraham all that the covenant will demand: succeeding generations would not take the same path as he did from the Tigris-Euphrates Valley to *Eretz Yisrael*, nor does God currently engage in direct dialogue with us over the fate of cities or sons. But there is much to be learned from Abraham's story and struggle about the nature of the *brit* and a Jew's relationship to it—that is, the demands of partnership and commitment. Readers of the Torah text learn not to walk away, even when they are confused by the demands placed upon them. They learn that the promise of fame and fortune can be costly or painful, that one must struggle to distinguish a faith in a better world from a fundamentalist fanaticism that murders one's own children. One learns from the Torah text that the *brit* is contentious and, like any relationship, it needs to evolve and grow. From its inception, the covenantal relationship between God and Israel took no predictable path.

OTHER VOICES

There are other voices in the Torah that tell different stories: those of the matriarchs of the Jewish people. These voices have been muted and often trivialized over the millennia. Often, we are content to give them archetypal poses, seeing them as less complex figures than the patriarchs. Sarah, in the rabbinical tradition, is described as pure and chaste, while Rachel passively weeps for her children. But the women who traverse the landscape of the Torah can provide alternative models of covenantal behavior from that of their menfolk, who find God in existential moments on mountain tops and by riverbanks. And while the children of Israel often seem to have lost the power of these female voices, the Torah notes that God listened well to these women.

Abraham fights with God to give the inheritance and mantle of leadership to his first son, Ishmael. That Abraham is confused about his heir should be no surprise, for earlier he had assumed that the role might be filled by his spiritually impoverished nephew, Lot, or his foreign servant, Eliezer. But

Sarah will fight vehemently to protect Isaac's place as covenantal heir, intuiting the crucial role her son will play within
the family and the Jewish people. Sarah serves as the eyes
and voice of God when Abraham is blinded by the societal
rules of primogeniture. In desperation, Abraham cries to God:
"O that Ishmael will live in your grace!" But God supports
Sarah:

> Sarah your wife shall bear you a son, and you shall name
> him Isaac, and I will maintain My covenant with him as an
> everlasting covenant for his offspring to come. (Genesis
> 17:19)

The theme of who will claim the covenantal inheritance
returns more vividly in the next generation, when Isaac is
deceived by Rebecca, his wife. But here, the Torah warns the
clear-eyed reader when it begins this tale: "Isaac was old and
his eyes too dim to see" (Genesis 27:1). There is no subtlety
in that verse. The verb *to see* describes the most powerful
sense possessed by human beings and we are told that Isaac
lacks it. The reader, however, immediately sees what Isaac
cannot: that the choice of his wild warrior son, Esau, is
doomed to failure. Rebecca, in whose womb the twin boys
Esau and Jacob struggled, instinctively knows that Jacob is
the rightful heir. When she tells Jacob to lie to his father, Jacob
resists. But Rebecca propels him forward with the words:
"Your curse, my son, be upon me! Just do as I say and go
fetch for me" (Genesis 27:13). The men are reduced to blind-
ness and fetching, while Rebecca determines the fate of her
sons and the Jewish people.

Rachel and Leah, the matriarchs of the next generation,
bargain over making love with their husband, Jacob, and the

inheritance rights due to them from their father. When confronted by her irate father, Rachel feigns menstruation, and he meekly retreats. These powerful women imitate God as they give names to their children, the twelve sons who will become the Jewish people.

In the following generation, the Torah introduces Tamar. She is the daughter-in-law of Jacob and Leah's son Judah, whose descendants ultimately will rule over the Israelites in *Eretz Yisrael* and who is the ancestor of almost all Jews. Tamar is widowed and abandoned by her husband's family, yet she is convinced that in her womb the heir of Judah must be nurtured. Tamar seduces Judah, an act the Torah will later condemn as incest, yet the Torah validates her violation of sexual norms as meritorious. From this incestuous relationship is born Perez.

Generations later, a Moabite woman leaves her family and homeland to return with her mother-in-law to *Eretz Yisrael*. The Moabites are descended from Lot, a weak man who was seduced by his own daughters because they feared that there were no men left in the world. Ruth, the Moabite, forces herself upon Boaz, himself a descendant of Judah and Tamar through the line of Perez. Ruth and Boaz become the ancestors of King David, from whose loins we are told the messiah will arise. This intricate genealogy, cherished and transmitted through the centuries, is at the heart of Jewish visions of redemption. Judaism and the community that observes its commandments must confront the tradition inherited from the Bible that the messiah will descend from the incestuous sexual encounter between Judah and his daughter-in-law, Tamar, and from their descendant Boaz, who married the forbidden foreigner, Ruth.

David Biale writes of Ruth, but the same could be said of Tamar, and even of the matriarchs and Esther:

> Ruth subverts sexual custom in order to secure her marriage to Boaz; only by bending the social norms can she win her destined mate and give fertility to the line of David. The erotic initiative in this tale falls, significantly, to women. . . . The Book of Ruth, therefore, at once reinforces and subverts patriarchy. Women play the critical role of ensuring fertility—a role perhaps dictated by patriarchy—but they do so by subversion of sexual custom.[3]

He then concludes with a new focus on the clearly affirmed yet antinomian role of women in the Bible:

> It is as if God must step backstage in order to make space for human actors, and particularly women, to bend social custom and law. . . . God's absence implicitly sanctions these inversions and subversions.[4]

What does one make of these stories of women who deceive their husbands, sons, and in-laws? Their stories are certainly found in the Bible, yet, unlike those of their husbands, there is no trace of their lives and faith in the liturgy of the Jewish people. They have been attacked as vicious and petty, selfish and cruel, or sanctified as pious and modest. These women all share a passion for increased life and for the expansion of the covenantal promise originally offered to Abraham alone. They battle with their wombs and their sexual skills because these are the only tools that have been given to these women of passionate commitment. They fight within and for the family, because their intuition tells them that the covenant is not simply an existential belief, but a family affair of blood and body. One wonders why a father who is willing to murder his son or another who abandons his family to wrestle with an angel are held aloft as models of faith while the women who struggle to bear children and protect their covenantal mission are seen as incidental.

Perhaps, in earlier ages, only part of the primal stories of the Jewish people could be heard. Yet, as with the DNA transmitted to the zygote, Jews inherit the experiences and memories of their mothers as well as their fathers. These biblical women are eloquent reminders that the traditions of Judaism speak in rich, vibrant, and contradictory voices. Today, in an era that allows for more varied roles for men and women and finds greater complexity in our understanding of gender, new readings of texts that have patiently gestated for well over three thousand years can unfold and guide the Jewish people. As Mordecai, the besieged Jew, will say to Esther, the queen who can save the Jewish people, in a story found near the end of the Bible, "Who knows, perhaps you have attained your position for just such a crisis" (Esther 4:14).

3

LIBERATION:
THE SUBVERSIVE PARADIGM

Imagine that something extraordinary occurs in your life. It may be an occasion for celebration or one of unbearable pain: you graduate with the highest honors; you witness the birth of your child or the death of your parent; you fight in a war or survive a near-death experience. Whatever it is, at the moment it happens, you recognize its importance and struggle to retain its vividness. The thought of losing the intensity of this moment is unthinkable, so you seek a way to make the memory meaningful forever.

Communities and cultures also strive to remember extraordinary moments in their past. Through the events remembered and the stories told about those events, each community also reveals what it values and offers its members answers to ultimate human questions.

Invariably, a community must relate how it came into being. Every people retains the memory of its own formation. The English tell their children how the Angles and Saxons conquered their island, and one leader—the ancestor of the present queen—was chosen as the bretwalda or ruler. Each year, in a variety of rituals and melodies, Christians retell the story of the death and resurrection of Jesus, the basic memory from which Christianity flows. Once there was a prince named Siddhartha who fled his family, wealth, and power to sit under a Bodha tree and achieve the perfect state of nirvana, and so unfolds the Buddhist story. Conquistadors from Spain fulfilled a prophecy when they built a city exactly where they saw an eagle carry off a snake in its beak, thus beginning the narrative of how Mexico City was founded.

For Jews, the extraordinary moment to remember and retell is the Exodus. The Israelites were slaves in Egypt, the Torah relates, and were liberated in a most miraculous fashion. That event and its ramifications will forever define Jewish identity and the role of Jews in the world.

Much can be learned about a people through the story it tells of its birth. What and how a people remembers reveals what it values and nurtures as a community. The story of the Exodus, although originally told about the Israelites, has been adopted by many peoples and nations as their own. Blacks sing of old Pharaoh and crossing the Jordan River from desert and slavery to freedom and happiness. Socialists saw the capitalist entrepreneur as the taskmaster and the workers as slaves to be liberated. The founders of the United States also relied heavily on biblical imagery to give meaning to their fight for freedom. In fact, the contrast between the ways that American culture and Jewish tradition utilize the same Exodus story can be instructive in clarifying how each defines itself and the power of memory in shaping their respective visions.

The founders of the United States needed a story that

would give meaning to the patriots' struggle against England. Their identification with the biblical Israelites fortified their contention that America was different from Europe; they considered the Old World's political system of monarchy and empire not only politically corrupt but also pagan. The Exodus story of the victory of the weak over the mighty and the triumph of freedom over domination inspired the colonial rebels in their own struggle against a mighty and domineering British Empire. Just as the Israelites stood behind Moses against the tyranny of Pharaoh, so the American patriots saw themselves rebelling against the absolute authority of the king of England. For them, the Exodus saga paralleled the history that began on July 4, 1776, and was completed when the British general Cornwallis surrendered to George Washington at Yorktown.

The Bible also provided the new nation with a sense of mission. The founders portrayed the United States as the modern manifestation of the Torah's vision of liberation. They saw themselves in the Promised Land, building a new civilization free of European evil and political corruption. The self-evident truths of the Declaration of Independence derived from the Bible's assertion that human beings were created in the divine image as God's partners with a mandate to change the world, and with no king save God. Ben Franklin thought the seal of the United States should be the children of Israel crossing the Red Sea, with the motto "Rebellion to tyrants is obedience to God." To emphasize their identification with the ancient Israelites, the colonies gave biblical names to many of their towns and cities.

The American story is a triumphant one, full of brave heroes and remarkable statesmen—from Washington to Jefferson, from Patrick Henry in Virginia declaring, "Give me liberty or give me death," to Nathan Hale regretting that he had but one life to give for his country. The American story begins with rebellion and ends with entry into the Promised Land. Independence is achieved, political rights are assured, and the triumph of freedom is complete. What follows is the contentment of success. It is this powerful and compelling story that propelled the nascent United States to its remarkable future.

Judaism begins its story with no victory and no song. A degraded and humiliated people, unable to do more than moan, is liberated by God almost against its will. From the shame of servitude, Israel the nation is born and its God becomes known in the dramatic opening words of the Ten Commandments: "I am the Lord your God who took you out of the land of Egypt, the house of bondage." God as liberator becomes the most significant divine attribute.

Judaism has the same story of freedom at its core as does the United States—but its retelling is fundamentally different. There is no human grandeur in this story, unless you count the peoples' frightened trudging into the desert as heroism. Moses is a reluctant leader whom God drags back to Egypt to assume his role. His brother, Aaron, is weak and petulant; his sister, Miriam, often petty. The Israelites are ornery and contentious, constantly doubting the reality of their liberty. Though they have witnessed a most miraculous liberation, the moment they face adversity, they cry: "Aren't there enough graves in Egypt that you brought us to the desert to die?" (Exodus 14:12). Liberation frightens them even more than Pharaoh did. They have no assurance in who they are and no confidence in their future. Moses repeatedly tries to make them realize that human beings ultimately are meant to be free, but they do not believe him. In spite of themselves, they march into the desert and wander for decades. This generation of the desert that witnessed the miracle of the Exodus, yet unable to accept freedom, will die there. The story of the Exodus, and the Torah itself, ends in the desert.

One can understand the power of these formative stories by observing how remarkably they still shape the self-image and conscious values of the communities that have absorbed them. Americans are raised to identify with the superheroes of the past, the confident warriors and articulate orators who symbolize American liberty and strength. We admire those men and women who strode through history never looking back, filled with the knowledge that their cause was just and their will unbreakable. The world is divided between the forces of good and the forces of evil, and our heroes are on the side of good. In this world, human beings not only have infinite potential, but they also believe that perfection is attainable now. North Americans have been brought up with little sense of self-doubt, struggle, or failure.

As the biblical story is transmitted in Jewish traditions, the liberation is just a beginning; it is but the first act in a continuous drama that will end in an ideal state of freedom in a perfect world. Liberated slaves do not became free men and women overnight. They only acquire a greater potential to live their lives as free men and women. Political freedom merely initiates a process that ultimately must go much deeper. There is no automatic leap into the Promised Land.

The stories a people tells and the meaning attributed to them deeply affect the choices that community will make. The rosy optimism of North Americans, their seeming unwillingness to grasp the incomplete state of human freedom, often seems dangerously naive. The Jewish insistence on the incomplete state of human freedom, on the other hand, can be criticized as cynical and bleak. In this case, how one re-tells the Exodus story colors the ways one works to change the world.

Jewish traditions caution against undue optimism regarding the human partnership with God. That may be why the Torah, at least the part that tells the story of the Israelites' birth and development as a people, begins and ends outside the Promised Land. If homecoming, that is, the arrival in the Land of Israel, constitutes a fulfillment of the vision, then the failure of Moses, Aaron, Miriam, and the entire generation of the Exodus to come home is a painful reminder that freedom from slavery is not enough. It seems strange that the most sacred text of the Jewish people should start with degradation and end with death in the desert. The more complete literary bracket to the Exodus from Egypt would be the entry into *Eretz Yisrael* found in the Book of Joshua.

Parallels abound with the Exodus story. Joshua succeeds Moses as the leader of the Israelites and leads them to the conquest of *Eretz Yisrael* even as Moses led them out of Egypt. Just as God initiates Moses into his role as leader on the sacred ground of the Burning Bush, so Joshua speaks with God on the sacred ground of the Land of Israel. The joyful crossing at the River Jordan into the Promised Land recalls the waters of the Red Sea that propelled the Israelites out of Egypt. The miraculous victory against Egypt is matched by the dramatic conquest of Jericho. Yet despite this perfect literary symmetry, the story of Joshua is not part of the Torah. The Torah ends with a rawer voice, on a tone of dissonance. The good news, it tells us, is that the Israelites were freed from Egypt; the bad news is that this people did not quite make it into the Promised Land. So much for happy endings.

The same tone is carried into Jewish tradition and into Jew-

ish storytelling. The tale of the Exodus, which Jews recount
to their children again and again, never quite achieves completion. Not only that, but in the retelling, the memory of
slavery virtually triumphs over that of freedom. The Torah
justifies its demand that the children of Israel focus on the
memory of slavery with the refrain "because you were slaves
in the land of Egypt."

> You shall not subvert the rights of the stranger or the father-
> less; you shall not take a widow's garment in pawn. Remem-
> ber that you were a slave in Egypt and that the Eternal your
> God redeemed you from there.
>   When you reap the harvest in your field and overlook a
> sheaf in the field, do not turn back to get it; it shall go to the
> stranger, the fatherless, and the widow. . . . Always remem-
> ber that you were a slave in the land of Egypt. (Deuteronomy
> 24:17-21)

The prophets who spoke to the Israelites in *Eretz Yisrael*
pushed the Exodus dream deeper into the future, insisting
that the people identify with the most degrading aspects of
their past. One of them, the prophet Jeremiah, who witnessed
the destruction of the Temple and the Jewish kingdom,
blamed this national tragedy on the people's failure to remember what it meant to be a slave.

The prophet Isaiah took this idea even further when he
declared that true freedom and homecoming would not be
complete until the Egyptians who enslaved Israel became
a blessing for the earth. On that day, Israel shall be a third
partner with Egypt and Assyria as a blessing on earth; for
the Eternal of Hosts will bless them, saying, "Blessed be My
people Egypt, My handiwork Assyria, and my very own
Israel" (Isaiah 19:24). According to this vision, even when

the Israelites of the Bible were living in *Eretz Yisrael*, they were not yet home and their freedom was not complete.

The Pesach Seder, instituted by the Rabbis living in *Eretz Yisrael* following the destruction of the Temple in 70 C.E., was constructed to allow Jews to reenact the transition from the degradation in Egypt to the celebration of freedom. In thousands of cities where Jews have lived in the nineteen centuries since the Rabbis, extended Jewish families have gathered around tables and recited: "In each and every generation one must feel as if he or she personally has just been redeemed from Egypt."[1] Yet all that really occurred in the Torah story is that the Israelites entered the desert. The homecoming is still out of reach. The liberation is not complete—at least, not yet.

What is going on here? Why this preoccupation with the memory of slavery while rejecting the wholeness of liberation? Is it not time that Judaism wholeheartedly embrace freedom and declare victory? Today, there is an independent Jewish state in *Eretz Yisrael*. Jews finally live in an era of ever-increasing democracy in nations that protect the rights of minorities. One wonders what psychic value is achieved by focusing on the humiliating story of a slavery in which God is so dominant, the people so abject, and true liberation remains only an unattainable ideal.

But this very focus, and the way it distinguishes its view of the state of its own liberation and that of the rest of the world, lies at the heart of Judaism. Americans declared that the revolution against England was to insure "life, liberty, and the pursuit of happiness," the right of every individual to live a life as unencumbered as possible by others and by the government. For Jews, on the other hand, to be unencumbered by a dominant political force is not the goal but the beginning. Liberation was not only "freedom from" slavery in Egypt, but also "freedom for" a distinct purpose: the demand "that you will remember all My commandments and will be sacred to your God" (Numbers 15:41). In the Torah's view, the antithesis of liberation is not only the physical pain of slavery but also the spiritual entrapment of paganism.

THE MEANING OF JUDAISM'S WAR AGAINST PAGANISM

The Torah makes clear that the purpose of liberation is to rid the world of corrupting idolatries that deflect men and women from the divine mission of improving human existence. To that end, the Torah directs the Jewish people to be implacable enemies of paganism. Its critique of the pagan world is at the heart of all traditions inherited by the Jewish people, another supporting pillar of Judaism.

For modern, open-minded men and women raised in a democratic culture, the unrelenting charge to destroy paganism may sound frightening. It raises the spectre of fundamentalist inquisitions, veiled women, and religious fanatics. As North Americans, we are encouraged to accept each other as we are, with all our flaws and inadequacies. The diversity of the world's people and our own multicultural society demand that we allow for infinite variations in human expression, including a spiritual potpourri that validates every mode of worship. In fact, in this environment, matters such as religion and politics are preferably left undiscussed, thought of as private issues that are not of public concern.

Not so Judaism, which demands the eradication of all vestiges of idolatry. Once liberated from slavery, the Israelites are commanded to wipe out those who practice certain other religions. "You shall destroy all the peoples that the Lord your God delivers to you, showing them no pity. And you shall not worship their gods, for that would be a snare to you" (Deuteronomy 7:16). There seems to be an unbearable tension here between the traditional injunction and our modern mores. A Judaism that is a source of extremism, a fueler of religious holy wars, is surely repugnant—contrary to what we regard as modern and humane. And yet, the connection between liberation and the attack on idolatry continues to define contemporary Judaism. The resolution of the tension again may lie in focusing on the Torah's intentions in its understanding of idolatry.

When we think about idolatry, we tend to imagine pagans bowing and offering sacrifices before statues of stone or wood or metal. We may focus on gruesome rituals such as the immolation of children to propitiate the gods or the erotic male and female prostitution that was a regular aspect of the Canaanite temple ceremonies. All of this sounds very primitive and completely alien to our own existence. But idolatry implies much more than bowing to graven images onto which the worshiper has projected supernatural powers. The pagan world knew that their gods did not actually reside in the idol. The Torah's attack on idolatry had less to do with the pagan forms than with the underlying beliefs of its world—beliefs that impede Judaism's contention that the world can be improved.

Consider the worship of the senior Canaanite god, Baal, for example. The actions of the god follow an annual cycle. In the summer, Baal is virile and productive as he copulates with the fertility goddess Asherah, who provides food to sustain the people. In the fall, the harvests are completed and rituals of thanksgiving are performed. In the winter, Baal dies and the earth lies fallow. In the spring, with festive ceremony, Baal is resurrected. In the text below, Baal's followers describe this predictable cycle of transitions from fertility to scarcity, from birth to death:

Baal impregnates the earth:

Now behold let Baal make fertile with his rains
   let him indeed make fertile with torrents and moisture.
Let him give forth his voice from the clouds,
flash to earth his lightening.[2]

As Baal meets Mot, god of death, in battle:

the olive tree is scorched
the yield of earth withers
and the fruit of trees.[3]

And so Baal dies:

Baal is dead: what of the people?
The son of Dagon: what of the multitude?[4]

Until victory is finally assured in Baal's rebirth:

Yours, O gods, behold
Mot is yours.[5]

In the story, Baal is known as king, because he restores food each year after the land has lain fallow; as the earth again turns green, the story remains compelling and meaningful. It is part of a pattern of regularity that parallels nature's own repetitive cycle. For the Canaanites, telling the epic of Baal is the best way to describe reality.

The world of paganism is deterministic; no change is possible, for the world is complete as it is. The gods themselves are regulated by natural cycles and forces of fate over which they have no control. Human life mimics nature with cycles and patterns returning upon themselves.

In the pagan world, human beings live preordained lives as part of a vast repetitive scheme—birth, growth, fertility, children, death. Through religious rites and propitiation of their gods, human beings seek harmony with the natural world. All human events are explained in the same way as are environmental changes (earthquakes, hurricanes, volcanic eruptions, or droughts)—as a warning that the world must be returned to its natural balance. None can claim either uniqueness or significance. In such a world, there is neither history nor progress, only eternally recurring cycles. Even as ancient civilizations fell, the idolatries thrived, while defeated empires and their gods were simply replaced by more powerful ones.

It was possible for the pagan world to contain many gods because, no matter how many there were, they still were not free. Ultimately, the gods had to bow to the absolute control of the natural world. If the gods themselves were controlled, how much more so were the people who served those gods. The hierarchies of the gods were mirrored in the human societies that worshipped them, where birth determined a person's status and fate. The societies of antiquity had kings and serfs, free men and slaves. A world of absolutes ruled: absolute monarchs, absolute political and religious and social systems. The Egyptian pharaoh was a veritable god, with the power to do to his subjects all that he willed. Ancient Greece may have instituted democracy among the elect few, but it also maintained a permanently enslaved underclass.

Judaism's war with paganism results from its fundamental and adamant opposition to the underlying notion of a world that cannot be changed or improved. Judaism bridles against paganism's support of absolutes—political and spiritual. Pharaoh and Caesar, Judaism declares, like nature itself, ultimately must be subservient to a force beyond human apprehension—the only absolute. Nations ancient and modern, built on the power of absolutes, have recognized Judaism's challenge.

The irony is that Judaism can only accept as absolute a God who is unknowable and whose will humans cannot fathom. Any community that claims temporal, this-world perfection is seen as engaging in a form of dangerous alien worship, because within their world there can be no purposeful change. Anyone who claims to "understand it all" is guilty of idolatry. Seen through this perspective, the Exodus wrenches human beings out of the rut of the repeating cycles of the pagan world into forward motion. It propels Israel into history with an acknowledgment that the world is not perfect, but with the belief that things can change, and that human beings can effect that change. And it declares that first, human beings must be free. The Exodus pushes humanity toward freedom, even if it does not yet provide the methods that will allow people to create a more perfect world. That will come later, at Mount Sinai.

The story of the Exodus becomes the fundamental paradigm of the Jewish people. Years later, in a world devoid of paganism, ideologies and leaders still arise who demand absolute loyalty. The Exodus challenges Jews to question the societies in which they live, including (as the prophets did) their own. Jews must always be aware that improvement is not only possible but mandated, because, in spite of claims to the contrary, the world is not yet perfect.

It is this tradition that makes Jews subversives. By asking questions, they challenge the absolutes around them. And that has been their historic role. Michael Lerner explains:

> Every ruling elite of the ancient and medieval world, and many in the modern world, justified their rule by ideologies whose central message was that the world cannot be changed. . . . Along came the Jews with a very different message: "The world can be fundamentally changed. Every system of oppression, no matter how powerful it appears to be, can be overthrown. . . . We know it, because we did it ourselves."[6]

The Maccabees fought against Antiochus, who claimed he was like a god. Later, Jewish rebels resisted the omnipotence of Roman power and world domination. In Europe, Jews rejected the divine rights of kings even as they denied the supremacy of the Catholic Church and of Islam. The mere existence of Jews repudiated the absolute truths by which Nazism attempted to control the world. And when Marxism was translated into a totalitarian absolute in the Soviet Union (which instituted an assault on all things Jewish), Jewish resistance helped bring about Communism's collapse there. Even in the United States and Canada, Jewish demands for equal status and full civil rights belied the assumption that these were two Christian nations. The Exodus model of revolution allows no one and no system to claim an absolute hold on truth.

4

Standing under the Mountain

The covenant with Abraham and Sarah encompassed one family; the covenant initiated at Sinai created—and ultimately embraced—an entire nation. The liberation from Egypt brought together separate tribes, as well as other individuals who had escaped slavery with the Israelites. Into the wilderness of Sinai marched this strange collection of men, women, and children, united only in their awareness of a miraculous delivery and in their fears.

Affirmation and Doubt: The Tensions of a New Relationship

There, still in shock over the freedom they are yet unable to comprehend, the former slaves find themselves led to a mountain afire with God's presence. They are told that God treasures them and wants to renew the forgotten covenant:

> The Lord called to [Moses] from the mountain, saying, "Thus shall you say to the house of Jacob and declare to the chil-

dren of Israel: 'You have seen what I did to the Egyptians, how I bore you on eagles' wings and brought you to Me. Now then, if you will obey Me faithfully and keep My Covenant, you shall be My treasured possession among all the peoples. Indeed, all the earth is Mine, but you shall be to Me a kingdom of priests and a sacred nation.'" (Exodus 19:3-6)

The Children of Israel answer immediately, "All that the Lord has spoken, we will do" (Exodus 19:8). In so doing, they affirm a partnership between themselves and God that is dedicated to perfecting the world, and they accept a uniquely Jewish method for living a meaningful life.

But the relationship at this point is far from ideal, and the contractual terms of the partnership still uncertain. The years of the desert are filled with anger and suffering, signs that the Israelites are wandering in confusion. While God's love and protection are evident to some (in the liberation from Egypt and the passage through the desert), most of Israel has little idea what "obey" and "keep My covenant" really mean.

The story of the desert overflows with the powerful tensions inherent in a relationship of complex love. There is God expressing jealousy and the hurt of rejection, and there are the Israelites chastising God for not knowing what they require and how to soothe their fears. The Torah's memory of the desert experience expresses both the magic and the difficulty of being in love. Few of us would marry if we anticipated in detail days and nights of sleeplessness, argument, and frustration. The American tradition of saying "I do" at the wedding ceremony is a commitment to relationship in spite of any difficulties the future may bring. So too with the ancestors of the Jewish people marching in the desert. They agree to be partners in a covenant without knowing the implications of the arrangement—that it may entail traumatic exiles, abiding guilt, and the death of their descendants in Jerusalem or Auschwitz.

Jon Levenson both focuses us on the tensions of this relationship and declares its centrality:

> There is, therefore, no voice more central to Judaism than the voice heard on Mount Sinai. Sinai confronts anyone who would live as a Jew with an awesome choice, which, once encountered, cannot be evaded—the choice of whether to obey God or to stray from him, or whether to observe the commandments or let them lapse. . . . In short, Sinai demands that the Torah be taken with radical seriousness. But alongside the burden of choice lies a balm that soothes the pain of decision. . . . The balm is the surprising love of YHWH for Israel, of a passionate groom for a bride, a love ever fresh and never dulled by the frustrations of a stormy courtship. Mount Sinai is the intersection of love and law, of gift and demand, the link between a past together and a future together.[1]

The sages, living one thousand years after the Exodus and always sensitive to nuance, recognized how hard was the bargain struck at Sinai. Thus, they tell this *midrash* to explain why Israel accepted the Torah at Sinai:

> It was not indeed quite of their own free will that Israel declared itself ready to accept the Torah, for when the whole nation . . . approached Sinai, God lifted up this mountain and held it over the heads of the people like a casket, saying to them: "If you accept the Torah, all is well, otherwise you will find your graves under this mountain."[2]

Yet even as the sages express skepticism about the completeness of Israel's faith, they accept the prophet Jeremiah's evocation of trust and devotion in the relationship between these newly freed slaves and God in the desert:

> Thus says the Lord:
> I will remember this of you,
> The caring devotion of your youth;
> the love of our wedding vows;
> how you went after Me into the desert,
> into the unsown wilderness. (Jeremiah 2:2)

Today, Jews invoke that affirmation when, during the synagogue service, the Torah is raised before the standing congregation, displaying the text that has served as the fundamental guide of the Jewish people. When the Torah is read, Jews link themselves to a chain of Jews through the generations who accepted these words as the basis for their lives. When the prayer taken from the Book of Deuteronomy, the *Shema*, is recited, declaring God's reality, the tradition declares that it is as if each listener is standing once again at Sinai, witnessing the covenantal moment in which God gave the gift of Torah. As the words from Proverbs and the liturgy record, "It is a tree of life to them that grasp it; all its paths lead to wholeness and peace" (Proverbs 3:18).

Of course, what exactly happened at Sinai is fraught with debate. For some, this is the pivotal question that determines their willingness to accept Judaism as true. For these people, without incontrovertible evidence of divine Revelation, belief and commitment are impossible. But to counter that position, it bears repeating that what and how one believes is always a choice. A person can choose to believe the evidence of his wife's love or can find proofs to the contrary; a person can believe that goodness and justice will triumph in the end or can find the proofs to conclude that evil always wins. No amount of data will convince you that you are esteemed if your heart directs you to feel worthless and painfully alone. Belief is inextricably connected to autobiography; faith is willed, not proven.

Gunther Plaut sensitively explains his own relationship to the events of Sinai:

> The foundations of Judaism as we have come to know them rest firmly on the tradition that the Eternal of history revealed Godself to one particular people and that in consequence of this revelation, and the compact which climaxed it, the people of Israel saw itself forever in the grasp of divine obligation. . . . They live forever on two planes that are yet one and the same, exposed to humans and nations with their demands and exposed to God's.[3]

Judaism stakes its claim on a person's acceptance of God's love through the revelation of sacred words.

For me, the story and traditions to which I commit my life rest firmly in the belief that what occurred at Sinai, handed down by my people as the Torah, is the core of my obligation to be a partner with God in redeeming the world. The Voice recorded at Sinai as heard by my ancestors is one which I search to hear in the words of the Torah and all the commentaries, debates, poetry, and laws that flow from it. I cannot prove that the event occurred with charts, videos, or other forms of scientific data. But then, all those aspects of life most important to me—love, empathy, hope, meaning, self-worth—cannot be proven with externally defined evidence. And yet it is the belief in these intangibles that creates, molds, and makes sense of my reality. Without these beliefs, as without my faith that God spoke to me at Sinai, life would not be worth living. This I share with those who stood at the foot of the mountain in the desert following their escape from Egypt.

And yet spiritual election does not lead to perfection in the aftermath of Sinai. The very chapters that describe the loftiness of the Israelites' response at Sinai also characterize them as rebellious and weak-willed. The giving of the Ten Commandments is immediately followed by the story of the Golden Calf. This serves as a reminder that partners in a relationship often fail to abide by the terms of their contract, no matter how great the initial love. It also underlines the continuing allure of idolatry, along with its concomitant fatalistic acceptance of the world's imperfections, seductive even to a people whose traditions state that they are elected by God. The contemporary philosopher David Hartman retells the *midrash*, which notes that the tablets broken by Moses following the apostasy of the Golden Calf were placed in the Ark of the Covenant along with the flawless tablets that Moses later brought down from the mountain,[4]

as if to say that God's reconfirmation of the covenant after the incident of the golden calf created a memory and awareness that human failure and rebellion are permanent possibilities of the covenantal relationship between God and the community.[5]

Hartman then concludes with the admonition:

The biblical description of Israel in the desert is a reminder not only of how vulnerable human beings are to idolatry, but also how willing they are to succumb to the attractions of slavery.[6]

THE FIRST COVENANTAL FAILURE

A new generation of Israelites enters *Eretz Yisrael*. Moses, the leader in the desert who constantly condemns the failings of the first generation of slaves made free, is not allowed to bring the children into the Land. But where their fathers and mothers failed, the new generation has every reason to believe it has succeeded in making the desert vision real, finally fulfilling the covenant of Sinai. Their victorious battles against idolatry clear the way for the promised community of God's servants. Life on the fertile land appears to confirm that God is with them. Eventually, as the city of Jerusalem is conquered and established as the national capital, God resides within the earthly abode of the Temple. The people periodically make a pilgrimage to the Temple in Jerusalem and prostrate themselves in awe as the priests offer their sacrifices and bless them. There is a ruling monarch who is descended from David, the poet-king.

To be an Israelite meant to live in *Eretz Yisrael*, obey the king, perhaps serve in his army, pay taxes and tithes, offer periodic sacrifices, and follow communal traditions such as *Shabbat*, the Holy Days, and certain dietary restrictions. And although the Israelite tribes eventually split into two separate kingdoms, one can assume that a sense of well-being and self-satisfaction existed in both. If the fulfillment of the covenant meant the promise of a rich life on the land, there was every reason for the kings, priests, and people to feel confirmed in the lives they led.

A successful, committed male Israelite would take the first fruits he harvested from the soil of the land which God had given and bring them in a basket to Jerusalem. There, he would deliver the basket to the priest in the Temple and recite a personal story that was, at the same time, the story of the people of Israel. With these words, each Israelite could invoke the sacred narrative, defining his own and the nation's self-identity:

> My father was a wandering Aramean. He went down to Egypt few in number and lived there, becoming a great and populous nation. The Egyptians dealt harshly with us, oppressed us, imposing heavy burdens. We cried out to the Lord, the God of our ancestors, and the Lord heard our plea and saw our suffering, our misery, and our oppression. The Lord freed us from Egypt by a mighty hand and an outstretched arm and awesome power, with signs and wonders. God brought us to this place and gave us this land, a land flowing with milk and honey. Therefore, I now bring the first fruits of the soil which You, O Lord, have given me. (Deuteronomy 26: 5-10)

Yet, if the Israelites and their leaders were convinced that they had fulfilled their part of the covenantal bargain, the prophets were not. At first, the voices of these outsiders were ignored and suppressed. The evidence of the good life clearly contradicted the anger and unrelenting condemnations of the prophets. God demands more than sacrificial animals, the prophets cried. The covenant demands that you care for the widow and the orphan, leave the corner of your fields for the poor, and treat the stranger with respect. If not, all that you treasure will be lost. If not, the covenant will be broken, and there will be no repair.

After he condemns the nations surrounding Israel for their brutalities (rape, pillage, murder, and genocide), the prophet Amos declared that Israel is accountable for its own sins as well. But Israel's sins are different. Because of their election by God, the prophet holds his fellow citizens to a standard of behavior and morality that is radically higher than that of its neighbors:

> Thus said the Lord:
> For three transgressions of Israel,
> For four, I will not revoke [my decree of destruction]:
> Because they have sold for silver
> Those whose cause was just,
> And the needy for a pair of sandals.
> [Ah], you who trample the heads of the poor
> Into the dust of the ground,
> And make the humble walk a twisted course!
> Father and son go in to the same girl,
> And thereby profane my sacred name.
> They recline by every altar
> On garments taken in pledge,
> And drink in the House of their God
> Wine bought with fines they imposed.
>
> (Amos 2:6-8)

When the growing empire of Assyria spills over the borders of *Eretz Yisrael* and consumes the northern kingdom of Israel, the survivors must wonder whether, perhaps, they should have listened more carefully to the prophetic voices.

When the Babylonian armies encircle Jerusalem, the king panics and heeds one appeal of the prophet Jeremiah. He moves to liberate the slaves. But it is too late. Babylonia cannot be stopped and soon the Temple, Jerusalem, and most of her inhabitants lay wasted. The moaning words of desolation and sorrow are read to this day in the books of the prophets and in Lamentations:

> Remember, O Lord, what has befallen us;
> Behold, and see our disgrace!
> Our heritage has passed to aliens,
> Our homes to strangers.
> We have become orphans, fatherless;
> Our mothers are like widows.
>
> Gone is the joy of our hearts;
> Our dancing is turned into mourning.
> The crown has fallen from our head;
> Woe to us that we have sinned!
>
> Because of this our hearts are sick,
> Because of these our eyes are dimmed:
> Because of Mount Zion, which lies desolate;
> Jackals prowl over it. (Lamentations 5:1-3, 15-18)

The rational thinker would have concluded from this destruction that here was indisputable proof that the covenant was broken and that there was no possibility of repair. Either God is infirm, or else God is so disenchanted with Israel that the divine face has turned away from them forever. But the revolutionary prophetic voices that earlier called for the destruction of the Israelite kingdoms now prophesy that God's love will outlast the anger over Israel's failures if only Israel would change its ways and return to God. It is possible for

God, they declare, to unilaterally repair the breach of the covenant. God did not abandon the terms of the contract, the
prophets insist; rather, God has sued Israel for noncompli-
ance, demanding that Israel reestablish the covenantal relationship. Michael Wyschograd explains that Israel's will to
continue in its relationship with God is animated by love in
spite of its failures, "because the ancient Jew felt God's love
for him and could therefore come to believe that his sins
would be forgiven without the Temple and its sacrifices."[7]
Repentance would animate Israel's return.

According to Jewish tradition, God's need for Israel was
too great to allow the partnership to die. That is how we can
understand the passage in the Book of Ecclesiastes, which
includes one of the first uses of the word *tikkun*, or repair.
There it is stated that everything, the good and the bad, is
dependent on God's will. The implication is that even though
Israel broke the terms of the covenant, God will unilaterally
act to redirect the fate of God's people and repair the world:

> Consider God's doing! Who can straighten [make a *tikkun*]
> what God has twisted? So in a time of good fortune enjoy
> the good fortune; and in a time of misfortune, reflect: the
> one no less than the other is God's doing. Consequently,
> human beings may find no fault with God. (Ecclesiastes
> 7:13-14).

During this stage in the history of the Jewish people, God
has the power to liberate as well as destroy. The same God
who could free Israel from slavery and cause the walls of
Jericho to tumble down could also cause the Assyrians and
the Babylonians to destroy Jewish life in *Eretz Yisrael*. While
Jews may be partners, at this juncture, they are but God's

servants and must pray that God will show a change of heart. In this first great era of the Jewish people, *tikkun* lies predominantly in the hands of God.[8]

One wonders what the average priest or Israelite did the day after the destruction of the First Temple. Some were taken to Babylonia, others remained in *Eretz Yisrael*, and a few fled to Egypt. It is hard to imagine how the people's faith in a loving God who protects Israel could survive the degradation they suffered. For the decades following the Destruction, a return to the Land seemed impossible, and many former citizens of the Israelite nation abandoned all connection to the God or people of Israel. A pattern of response emerges: in every age, partnership in the covenant will be too painful or too problematic for many of the descendants of Abraham and Sarah to bear. Life is more realistic and less disappointing when lived as part of the victorious and powerful majority. Michael Lerner amplifies this awareness:

> From the very beginning of our history, Jews have been trying to run away from the responsibility and the terror of being witnesses to the possibility of healing and transformation.[9]

The majority of Jews still seem to flee from such a frightening task.

Yet, within the lifetimes of many of those who went into exile, the words of the prophets were confirmed and the new ruler of the Middle East, the king of Persia, allowed the Jews to go back to *Eretz Yisrael*. A small remnant returned; the Temple in Jerusalem was rebuilt, and the sacrificial cult was reinstituted. It is ironic that just at this point in Jewish history, as the prophetic promise of return is fulfilled and the prophets begin to be honored, the mode of prophecy—the word of God spoken directly to human beings—comes to an end. There no longer will be literary prophets who speak in God's name. The Jewish people, bereft of God's Voice, will be more on their own than ever before.

Five hundred years later, with the destruction following the war against the Roman Empire, the story will conclude differently. There will be no triumphant Jewish return to the Land, no rebuilding of the Temple in Jerusalem, and no renewed Jewish state. In the days before the Second Temple goes up in flames, a priest sacrifices the last animal, the final blessings are delivered and the last Jewish king pleads with the zealous rebels to surrender. A chapter is closed.

What does this suggest about the covenant and the relationship between God and the people of Israel that were in the desert? If the covenant could only be realized in the harvesting of the produce of *Eretz Yisrael*, in bringing gifts and sacrifices to the Temple and its priests, and in experiencing God's presence in that Temple, then the covenant was no more. Now there was no prophetic voice to speak in God's name and promise renewal. For many, exile and silence revealed a final, painful truth: that the fiery promise of a demanding God at Sinai to carry an obedient Israel on eagles' wings to the Promised Land and make her a treasured possession, "a kingdom of priests and a sacred people," was over. This catastrophe could not be repaired.

The historian Josephus Flavius initially was a Jewish general in the revolt against Rome. But when he joined the Romans against the Jewish rebels, he became a chronicler of their defeat. At one point, he stood outside the gates of Jerusalem and called on the people inside to surrender. Basing his plea on the Jewish tradition that only God can repair the damage and that God's defection was apparent, Josephus told his people how futile was their stand, that Roman power was invincible, that

> Fortune, on all accounts, has gone over to [the Romans]. God, having gone round all the nations within God's dominion, is now settled in Italy.
>
> O miserable creatures. Are you so dense about true support that you fight the Romans with your weapons and your hands? When did we ever conquer another nation by such means? And when did God, who is the creator of the Jewish people, not avenge us? Listen to me and know that we are not fighting against the Romans, but against God. God has fled from the Sanctuary and stands on the side of those against whom you fight.[10]

God seemed to be on the side of Rome.

5

Entering the Wilderness Once Again: The Perfection of the Rabbis

With the loss of the prophet's voice, the High Priest's Temple service, and the king's authority, God's will and word seemed impossible to locate. With no king, there could be no clear rule of Jewish law. With the physical residence of God in ruins, there was no place to sacrifice. And with all political power in the hands of the victorious Romans, there were no clear rules of behavior to follow. With no experience in how to believe and act as a Jew under these altered circumstances, assimilation or paralysis appeared for many to be the only choices.

There was a different, minority view, however: that of the sages who were called the Rabbis. The rabbi was a teacher. To become a rabbi, one had to study and learn the Torah and its traditions. Unlike priests and kings, any male Jew could become a rabbi, thus opening Jewish leadership to the most capable men. That leadership ability was evident immediately after the destruction of the Second Temple.

These sages did not retreat from history, but immersed themselves in retelling it in ways that directed Jewish renewal. Jon Levenson speaks of the theological implications of the Torah's rendition of history, which the Rabbis grasped in their hands and molded. The Torah, he claims, provided:

> A grounding that comes not from introspection or philosophical speculation, but from the recitation of a story. Telling the story brings it alive, actualizes it, turns it from past into present and bridges the gap between individual and collective experience, by enabling Israelities of the present generation to become the Israelites of the covenant, the Israel of the classic normative relationship with God.[1]

The Rabbis were superb storytellers.

Deeply committed to the continuity of the covenant between God and Israel, the Rabbis struggled to make sense of the catastrophes that had struck *Eretz Yisrael* and the Jewish people. Unlike the prophets who spoke in the days of the First Temple, the Rabbis sought no miracles of divine intervention nor were they willing to bear complete responsibility and guilt for the Destruction. Their response was most complex: It was to accept God's will while, at the same time, questioning the God who sat silent, seemingly brooding over the terrible events. See, for example, their comments on the words of the Torah that proclaim God's victory over the Egyptians: "Who is mighty like you, O Lord?" In their own time, the Rabbis taught, one should read:

> Who is like You, mighty in self-control? You heard the blasphemy and the degrading insults of that wicked man, but You keep silent! In the school of Rabbi Ishmael it was taught: Read mighty [the Hebrew word *elim*] rather as *illmim* [Who

is like you among the *mute*] since God sees the suffering of God's children and remains silent.[2]

To give meaning to Jewish lives shorn of much that had previously provided that meaning, the Rabbis reread the Torah texts and located many traditions that did not demand a Temple, a king, or even *Eretz Yisrael*. When asked how one could reach God or be cleansed from sin without the Temple sacrifice, the Rabbis focused on other behaviors and beliefs that could express a uniquely Jewish way of life:

> Once, when Rabbi Yohanan Ben Zakkai was leaving Jerusalem, Rabbi Joshua was walking behind him and saw the Temple in ruins. Rabbi Joshua said, "Woe is us that this has been destroyed, the place where atonement was made for the sins of Israel." [Rabbi Yohanan replied] "No, my son, do you not know that we have a means of making atonement that is like it? And what is it? It is deeds of love, as it is said, 'For I desire kindness and not sacrifice.'"(Hosea 6:6)[3]

Perhaps the Rabbis' brave awareness that God would not redeem them as God had done at the Red Sea forced them now to demand a greater human role in the *tikkun* of the world. The new conditions begged that someone speak in God's name—even as the voice of God no longer could be heard directly. So the Rabbis decided that they could and must decipher God's will. (See *Baba Metzia* 59b.)

The Rabbis refused to accept that the story of the Jewish people, its mission and vision, had died, and they constructed the means to move the story forward. With great internal debate and remarkable diversity, they rewove the strands of their people's story into a version that could withstand the suffering and disappointment that they and their fellow Jews had experienced. As the Rabbis patiently explained, the painful condition of destruction and exile destroyed neither the covenant nor the Jewish people. Now, according to the Rabbis, Jews could go anywhere on earth and remain Jews. Free from the limited physicality of the Temple and *Eretz Yisrael*, each Jew could be a partner in the covenant by fulfilling the many rituals and behaviors provided by the Rabbis. These behaviors, which commit Jews to live covenantally, are called *mitzvot*.

From the moment an observant Jew awakened in the morning until asleep at night, his or her life could be made sacred through these *mitzvot*. In this way, the Rabbis were able to speak of a personal *tikkun*, and a new relationship with God. Ridding oneself of sin and following the *mitzvot*—personal acts of healing—was something God desired, they explained, but could not control without the participation of human beings. Fulfilling *mitzvot*, then, could provide every Jew, as well as the entire Jewish community, with a way to find meaning in their lives: by seeing themselves both as obedient servants and yet fuller partners with God.

More important, these behaviors could help bring wholeness to the world. Thus, the Rabbis spoke of setting the time of prayer or structuring the Holy Days by using a derivation of the word *tikkun*. (See *Rosh HaShanah* 1:3.) To bring order into the world was not only a human possibility, but a human obligation. God could encourage and validate, but would not intervene.

The Rabbis had to reaffirm a covenant in a spiritually shattered setting, a world of great fear and loneliness. They did this by substituting personal *tikkun* for the national ones that had been lost. If they could not take political control of their world, they could assert control over the entire universe by claiming the sole right to determine time. And if they could not stop persecution and attacks against Jews, they could assert control by staying pure in the face of such evil. While no Rabbi would have voluntarily chosen this new life over one where an autonomous Israel could celebrate at the Temple in Jerusalem with priests and kings, the Rabbis' search for a way to do God's will enriched the soul and the spirit of the Jewish people with new meaning by constructing vibrant traditions for the individual, the family, and the community.

ISAAC LURIA: A NEW UNDERSTANDING OF TIKKUN

Over the next thousand years, individual Jews trudged into the most distant places with not much more on their backs than the traditions of *miztvot* and the belief that God loved them. Small Jewish communities sprang up in a multitude of lands, from Afghanistan to Tunisia, from the Rhine River Valley to Yorkshire, England, and deep into the steppes of Russia. Jewish families codified their own customs of foods to eat and songs to sing and how to marry off sons and daughters. In some places, Jews reached the heights of power, wealth, and prestige. There were Jewish prime ministers in North Africa and generals in Spain; there were court doctors in Egypt and financiers in Germany. Yet this world was fragile indeed, as Crusades, pogroms, and expulsions forced Jews to move from land to land.

During these long centuries, the Rabbis and the people kept alive the story of renewal, God's love, and the role of Jews as a chosen people obedient to God. They continued to nurture the system of *mitzvot*, finding new ways to fulfill God's will through study, prayer, and righteous acts. For many moderns today, the details of religious expression during these centuries may appear overly rigorous and demanding. But for the Jews of the medieval period, Jewish law and tradition were as natural as breathing in and out.

In particular, the Jews of Spain achieved remarkable successes during these years. Since Spain was divided between the Christian north and the Muslim south, Jews were needed as allies by both. Often Jews served as intermediaries, linking the two parts of the Iberian Peninsula. In that role, many Jews became important officials of the various Spanish governments. The Jewish community became known for its wealth and influence as well as for its scholarship and cosmopolitan character.

Then, during the fourteenth century, the rising power of the Catholic monarchies in Spain helped create an anti-Jewish and anti-Muslim attitude. Soon, there were violent attacks against Jews throughout the Iberian Peninsula. On New Year's Day, 1492, King Ferdinand and Queen Isabella marched triumphantly into the last Muslim stronghold of Grenada as the ruling Muslim khalif sailed across the Strait of Gibraltar to North Africa. The khalif had surrendered only after Ferdinand and Isabella signed an agreement protecting all the Jews in Grenada. But the new Catholic monarchs ignored their commitment and expelled all Jews and Muslims from Spain. By 1498, there were no Jews living publicly in the entire Iberian Peninsula (although Jews continued to live there secretly for centuries).

The entire Jewish world was rocked by the expulsion and destruction. Tens of thousands died, up to one half of Spanish Jewry converted, voluntarily or by coercion, and a great community and culture were destroyed. Many of the converts were subsequently tortured by the Inquisition. The catastrophe shook Spanish Jews to the core of their Jewishness. In their attempt to comprehend God's will in the events that had befallen them, many Spanish Jews were drawn to the mystical traditions of Judaism that had been present but not normative during much of Jewish history. And a small group of refugee Spanish mystics settled in the town of Tzefat in *Eretz Yisrael* during the middle of the sixteenth century.

These mystics reasoned that, as *shutafei Hakadosh Barukh Hu*, covenantal partners with God who were created in God's image, they must be blamed for the destruction. In a radical development of the concept of *tikkun*, the rabbis of Tzefat claimed that they could be the source of the rejuvenation as well. If only they were able to understand and correct their own failures, they believed, they could help redeem the world. Isaac Luria arrived in Tzefat in 1570 and died there in 1572. In those two years, he became the teacher and spiritual guide of the community. During that period, he also revolutionized the Jewish understanding of *tikkun*. In significant ways, a Judaism committed to social and political change is his spiritual legacy.

Rabbi Luria, known as *HaAri* (the Lion), taught that when God created the universe, there was so much divine energy that the earthly vessel shattered, leaving shards of light scattered around the world. Thus, embedded in the earth were millions of broken pieces of divine light. This sense of brokenness was so strong, Luria said, that God was, so to speak, broken as well. The Divine Presence, called the *Shekhinah*, was thrust into exile, just as Israel was thrust into exile. The world was now filled with shattered pieces of divine light, a wandering *Shekhinah*, and a suffering Israel in exile.

This interpretation of events was not so revolutionary. It was, from the perspective of medieval Jewish history, a pretty obvious statement of Jewish reality. What was most revolutionary, however, was Isaac Luria's idea that human beings were responsible for the *tikkun*, the repair of the shattered world. The covenantal task of the Jew, according to Luria, was nothing less than to pick up the scattered sparks of the Divine Presence, one at a time. Theoretically, if Jews worked hard enough and dedicated their lives to this task, they could complete the *tikkun* and bring on the redemption of the world. Every act completed, every thought, every breath taken could either bring the world closer to that *tikkun* or thrust it deeper into the chaos and ugliness of the world's brokenness. There were no neutral players in this scenario. One was either a force for goodness or for evil.

The rabbis living in Tzefat created pious customs in order to help refine themselves. The following excerpts are from Isaac Luria's own customs of self-improvement:

The most crucial of all worthy traits demand that an individual behave with humility, modesty and with the fear of sin as much as possible. One should also strive to keep good distance from haughtiness, anger, hubris, foolishness and gossip; even provoked, one should refrain from behaving harshly.

Before an individual begins to pray, that person must take on the commitment, "You shall love your neighbor as yourself." That person should focus on loving every member of the house of Israel, on account of which the prayers will go up, bound up with all the prayers of Israel. By this means, the soul will be able to rise above and effect Tikkun.

My Master, of blessed memory, took great care to avoid destroying any insect, even the tiniest and most insignificant among them, such as fleas and gnats, bees and such, even if they annoyed him.

My teacher, of blessed memory, used to tell me that . . .
all mental concentration must be focused toward binding
and uniting one's soul to its supernal source through Torah.
. . . For this is God's purpose in creating human beings and
God's intention in commanding them to study Torah.[4]

In Luria's construct, evil impulses can be imagined as fes-
tering wounds that infect everything that comes into con-
tact with them. When a person acts on these impulses, he or
she sins, blocking the ability to bring greater goodness into
the world. A person's actions produce negative vibrations that
are felt throughout the universe. The battle within is an endless one; the evil impulse is always in competition with the
desire to move closer to God and heal the broken world. The
rabbis of Tzefat explained that Judaism and the *mitzvot* are
the most effective tools to conquer the evil potential inside
and promote wholeness and healing. Remorse over sin, in
the form of penitential acts, could help purify the soul and
thereby allow a person to effect the necessary *tikkun* of the
world.

RABBI LURIA'S LEGACY

Through the teachings of Rabbi Luria, Jews asserted more
than control over the calendar and the internal life of the
community. They now could insist that the victories of Spanish kings, powerful sultans, and earthly popes were trivial.
They knew that the Jewish people could bring redemption,
whatever the political realities—if only each Jew was fully
committed to complete *tikkun*.

The eighteenth-century *chasidim* were among the heirs of

Rabbi Luria. They exploded through Europe with the message that redemption is possible through personal purification and the fear and love of God. One of the most fascinating of the chasidic *rebbes* was Nahman of Bratislav, who spoke in parables while leading his followers to a *tikkun klali*—the complete *tikkun* of the *tzaddik*, a wholly righteous human being. If only each human being would rid himself or herself of sin and follow a simple path, he taught, the covenant promised to Abraham and Sarah and to their descendants finally could be fulfilled:

> The sins of humans are very many. To correct each one individually is an overwhelming task. It is impossible to repent and rectify them all. We must rectify the array . . . as a whole. We do this through *Tikkun HaBrit*, a repair and strengthening of the Covenant. Sustaining the Covenant is therefore a remedy for all sin.
>
> The *Brit* is the foundation of the Jewish people's closeness to God in heaven. Keeping the Covenant is the *Tikkun HaKlali*, the complete *Tikkun*.[5]

Still, the physical condition of Jews and of the Jewish people deteriorated. All the piety and devotion to spiritual wholeness could not alter the painful reality of Jewish suffering and denigration. From a high point of perhaps as many as seven million Jews during the first century of the Common Era, there were probably under a half-million Jews left in the early 1600s.[6] As the world entered the eighteenth century and a modern dawning, the Jews of Europe were slipping into impoverishment and despair.

6

FACING MODERNITY

Physical suffering has been part of the human condition for so long that pain alone is seldom enough to drive people to improve the quality of their lives. People in traditional societies have often perceived change as too dangerous, the risks and potential losses too great. Tradition, the metaphor for continuity that defines oneself and one's purpose in life, provided more than solace for the Jews of the early eighteenth century. Tradition reminded them daily that the universe was in order and that each person had a place within it. By accepting those inherited traditions, a Jew was insured a life of meaning.

BREAKING THE CONNECTION TO THE PAST

This was a time in which the course of a man's life was quite predictable. Few would travel more than ten miles from their place of birth in an entire lifetime. Most likely, a man would follow the profession of his father, marry someone from the community and of the same religion, and live happily ever after. Names such as Smith or Carpenter, Schneider or Cohen, recurring on a family tree, give us the basic information about the lives of those men generation after generation. A woman's story would be just as predictable, except that she would bear children and stay at home. I can trace my family back to the 1600s in a few small German towns. For generations, my ancestors were cattle dealers, buying from and selling to their Christian neighbors. Their traditions were sustained through a reliable, unchanging network of family and communal structures.

Judaism, too, was dependent on this predictability. With all the pogroms and ghettoes, the Jews of Europe were still permitted to establish internal autonomy. Religion regulated the content and parameters of their daily lives. Early on, children were taught what they could and could not do. Rabbis and communal elders made sure that everyone conformed to the rules. Only scholars could question the meaning of the traditions or the sources of the laws. The rest of the community was taught that the Torah is true, the tradition is God's word, and that servants of God are commanded to obey. The certainty of a world rich in a sense of mission and a coherent rhythm of daily life may sound compelling to moderns who are beset with so many choices and moral alternatives. In those times, most everyone married and had families. Elderly parents were cared for by their children, the suicide rate was extremely low, and there was little need for therapists. If asked, these Tevyes and Goldas would have described the sense of purpose that permeated their lives in one word: tradition. In the premodern world, Judaism was part of the natural rhythm of a person's life, dwelling in harmony with the needs of individual, family, and community.

Personal choice and autonomy were not pressing issues during this period. While Judaism seeks to give meaning to the life of the individual and sees each human being as unique and of infinite value, these values were expressed within the context of a sacred community committed to fulfilling the will of God as determined by the rabbis. Prayers were recited in plural; liturgical requests were made in the name of the entire community. Even in the most intimate moments of Yom Kippur, when Jews sought to atone for a long list of personal wrongdoings, they were instructed to recite each confession in the plural, "For the sin which we committed. . . ."

The Torah records and Jewish traditions confirm that a person is defined through his or her web of relationships (as child and parent, sibling and cousin, member of a tribe and a people), but seldom as an existential being alone in the world or facing God. This principle is behind the custom of calling a Jew to the Torah by his or her father's given name (and in some synagogues, the mother's name as well). A Jew is a Cohen, Levi, or Israel—linked to the tribes that composed the Israelites three thousand years ago. To be a participant in the covenant is not a choice, Jewish tradition maintains, but a factor of birth (even the convert must be "reborn," not simply into the religion of Israel, but also into the family of Abraham and Sarah).

The closer the approach to the modern age, the greater were the breaks from these patterns of familial and communal continuity. Epidemics, wars, the exploration of the Americas, religious revolts, and scientific discoveries all pushed people out of the close network of home and community into a radically new world. The shift in social patterns was most obvious in North America. No matter how much the immigrant colonists to the United States or Canada may have tried to reconstruct the communities they knew in Europe, the flush of possibilities in the New World challenged any one group's demand for complete allegiance. The sociology of the modern age broke the bonds of communal obligation.

The sense of community was also undermined from another source: the radical philosophical ideas of the eighteenth and nineteenth centuries. It may seem strange to assert that an idea has the power to threaten a society. Certainly, an idea should have little power to change people who are living contentedly. Yet ideas can radically alter the way one sees the world—and, in so doing, turn contentment to rage. A slave who assumes that her master owns her has no impulse to resist her oppression. But teach her to believe that no human should ever be owned by another, and she suddenly will see a world of different possibilities. She may revolt, even if success is not assured. Similarly, a worker may have thought that he was satisfied to labor ten hours a day for six days each week. Once he accepts the idea that no man should work so hard, his happiness may turn to anger, even violence. By making people understand their pasts and their present circumstances differently, ideas allow them to anticipate an alternative future. America was a dazzling example of this.

The United States was founded on classical liberal principles documented in the Declaration of Independence and the Constitution of the United States. These principles proclaimed the revolutionary ideas that human beings have unalienable rights, that a community is governed for and by the people, and that the government's responsibility is to protect the rights and freedoms of each citizen. A correlate purpose of the community, as codified in the Declaration of Independence, was to maximize the potential of each of its members:

> We hold these truths to be self-evident, that all men are cre-
> ated equal, that they are endowed by their Creator with cer-
> tain unalienable Rights, that among these are Life, Liberty,
> and the pursuit of Happiness.

The limitations placed on the government, representing the community, are most apparent in the first amendment to the Constitution, declared in force on December 15, 1791. This first guarantee of the Bill of Rights protects individual freedoms:

> Congress shall make no law respecting an establishment of
> religion, or prohibiting the free exercise thereof; or abridg-
> ing the freedom of speech or of the press; or the right of the
> people peaceably to assemble and to petition the Govern-
> ment for a redress of grievances.

Both the physical realities of the North American continent and the political choices of its new settlers created an environment that broke down old assumptions about authority and monolithic truths. The expansiveness and richness of the land allowed pioneers to strike out on their own, homesteading tracts of fertile acreage. With such abundance, there was little need to form the closed, walled cities ruled by a prince or duke that were common in Europe at the time. In a country without an established national religion, no single force in society could declare absolute moral truths. And where a polyglot population of immigrants made up the citizenry, as they did both in the United States and Canada, the claim of a single inherited tradition was impossible. By definition, then, these two countries became communities of choice, with the tacit understanding that, by the will of the people and for the sake of the people, anything and everything could be changed. In contrast to the old ways of Europe, America exuded the vigor of a new attitude that celebrated personal liberation and independence.

The ideals of a society are often expressed in the legends of its heroes and heroines. In North America, a certain personality type emerges from the earliest stories of the continent's exploration. Henry Hudson sailed into Canada, fought the elements and a rebellious crew, and ultimately died alone. Frontier trappers, who were committed to no single town or community, mapped the rivers they forded and mountains they climbed by themselves. Davey Crockett and Daniel Boone left their homes to fight for justice and conquer the West, each by himself. Pioneer women were admired for their complete self-reliance and the isolated lives they led. Even the fighters of the Revolutionary War fit the model of the individualistic hero: Paul Revere, legend relates, rode off alone into the night to warn of the imminent British attack.

In North America, the political structures succeeded in promoting individuality and the right to pursue one's own happiness. The richness of American culture, the product of an array of immigrant traditions, created an environment in which newcomers could achieve great material success. But the principles that placed individuality above governmental or religious coercion also propelled personal experimentation, which in turn led to the breakdown of traditions. Within an environment of pluralism and freedom, most immigrant communities soon lost their distinctiveness. Their hyphenated identity as Americans of foreign extraction belied the larger reality: the passions and commitments of their past cultures were being abandoned for the vitality of America.

With new ideas, possibilities, and structures defining the modern age, religion did not fare well. Ideas that merely tried to reconstruct the past were of no help in resuscitating it; they could not make ancient traditions relevant to the world of new choices. Religion, and Judaism in particular, seemed to be a collection of rules that essentially answered all questions with a resounding "No!" One cannot eat this food. It is forbidden to drive a car on the Sabbath. Starve on certain days of the year, and do not dare touch bread on Passover. Keep your hands off your girlfriend, a youth is instructed, while a rabbi even presumes to tell married adults when they can and cannot have sexual intercourse. Many Jews began to view Judaism as a religion of negation, of abstinence and unrelenting sacrifice, handed down from generation to generation. To be a Jew was to become another link in this morose tradition.

From Religious to Revolutionary

In this atmosphere, it was difficult to identify with the Lurianic preoccupation with sin and evil or to adopt the sense of calm that derived from the constants of tradition. Yet modern Jews *could* relate to the revolutionary impulse in Judaism, which echoed the belief and mandate they had inherited from ancient and medieval Judaism proclaiming that each person could make a difference in the world. The idea became separated from its religious aspect, even as it fired a revolutionary zeal among those who had absorbed it in the teachings of their tradition. As moderns, we generally assign the task of repairing the world to eccentric scientists, mercurial political activists, artistic geniuses, and prescient industrialists. We don't believe that religious acts and fervent rabbis do really affect change. That is because, as children of modernity, we were taught by the American and French Revolutions to see the *secular* world as the sphere of change. We have become great believers in change—and yet, for Jews, these ideas are inherited from an older heritage.

Still, although the message of medieval Jewry had been that human beings can repair the world through religious piety, modern Jews were skeptical. The old order, it seemed to them, had suppressed freedom, creativity, and human rights. Sitting behind ghetto walls or cloistered in impoverished *shtetls* seemed a poor way to transform the world. While there were some who argued that the Jewish task is to wait patiently for the messiah to redeem them, most Jews were drawn to the revolutions sweeping across Europe and North America. They learned to translate the spiritual message into the secular arena: Created in God's image and bearers of the covenant, they must actualize the ultimate, complete *tikkun* through secular means. With visions of a redeemable world, Jews entered the nineteenth century.

7

JEWISH REENTRY INTO HISTORY

The last hundred years make up but a small percentage of the scope of Jewish history. Yet the Holocaust and the birth of the modern State of Israel take a disproportionate place in the overarching story of the Jewish experience. True, these events have a special intensity because many who experienced and witnessed them are still alive today. However, that is not the only reason for their tremendous influence on Jewish life and thought. It is clear that this world, and the Jewish world in particular, would be far different had there been no Auschwitz in 1944 nor the establishment of the State of Israel in 1948. Indeed, the forces of nineteenth-century modernism seemed to be pointing to an entirely different future. While it is hard to imagine such a world, it is important to try to recreate what could have been.

TRANSLATING *TIKKUN* INTO THE MODERN AGE

As the French Revolution swept across Europe, Jews rallied to its call for "Liberty, Equality, and Fraternity." So strong was their yearning to be part of the great enterprise of emancipation, so compelling was the pledge of equality and the promise of access to all that was beautiful and true, that when the French Revolution offered its Jews citizenship, they accepted wholeheartedly. The fine print, articulated by Count Clermont-Tonnere in 1791, was lost on these Jews who were enraptured by the proposed new freedoms. In France's debate over the emancipation of the Jews, Clermont-Tonnere convinced his compatriots to support Jewish rights with the words: "One must refuse everything to the Jews as a nation but one must give them everything as individuals; they must become citizens."[1] In other words, Jews could preserve particular practices and attend religious services as they wished—as long as they joined the community of French Revolutionaries. Any notions of an autonomous Jewish community or a separate allegiance to the Jewish people would have to cease. It was on this basis that the Jews were enfranchised in France and, over the century, achieved citizenship throughout Europe. The confusion between what the Christian majority meant by emancipation and what Jews understood it to be was never resolved, perhaps not until the Holocaust. Arthur Hertzberg clarifies: "The outline of all modern versions of the 'Jewish question,' as it was to be defined in the future by both Jews and gentiles, existed in 1791. The glories and the tragedies to come had already been conceived."[2]

Not everyone agreed with those who enthusiastically joined the French Revolutionaries. There were Jews who saw in it only the lurking danger to Jewish religious observance. The first Lubavitcher *Rebbe*, living in Imperial Russia during Napoleon's attack, was reputed to have said that he would support the czar against the French: The czar hurts our bodies but leaves our souls intact, he explained; the French Revolution will protect our bodies but destroy our souls. Another famous rabbi, the Chatam Sofer, with a play on a familiar rabbinic expression, said: "All that is new is forbidden by the Torah." Even so respected a thinker as the German rabbi Samson Raphael Hirsch balked at such a wholehearted affirmation of modernity and removed his followers from the organized progressive Jewish community and its non-Orthodox leaders:

> We declare before heaven and earth that if our religion demanded that we should renounce what is called civilization and progress we would obey unquestionably, because our religion is for us truly religion, the word of God before which every other consideration must give way. We declare equally that we would prefer to be branded fools and do without all the honor and glory that civilization and progress might confer on us rather than be guilty of the conceited mock-wisdom which the spokesman of a religion allied to progress here displays.[3]

But these leaders were in the minority. Where emancipation and enlightenment were offered, Jews enthusiastically joined the forces of change, helping to demolish the status quo in every area they touched. In the two hundred years since 1791, they consistently marched with the forces that offered freedom, and, as democratic forces prevailed, particularly in North America, they increasingly became part of the mainstream. Still, if there was great passion in their embrace of the idealistic movements, there also was great ambivalence about their own heritage. The Hebrew poet Tchernichowsky described the unbearable tension in the encounter between a seemingly anachronistic Judaism and vigorous and powerful modernity. In his poem "Standing Before the Statue of Apollo," a Jew confronts the future and cries:

I come before you, before your statue and I bow.
Your statue—symbol of light and life.
I bow, and bend the knee to the good and elevated.
I bow to life, to heroism, to beauty
I will bow to all the exquisite treasures, that corpses and rotten
    seeds of men have stolen.
Rebels against life—from the hand of Shaddai my Rock, the God
    of miraculous desert,
The God of those who conquered Canaan in a storm
They bound and tied God in straps of *tefillin*.[4]

In 1807, Napoleon convened an august gathering of Jewish leaders, both the preeminent rabbis of the Empire and its notables. The gathering was called the *Sanhedrin*, recalling the great assembly that determined Jewish law when Jews were autonomous decision-makers in *Eretz Yisrael*. The Emperor asked the assembled Jewish leaders a series of questions about their role as French citizens. They responded eagerly:

> Yes, France is our country; all Frenchmen are our brethren, and this glorious title, by raising us in our own esteem, becomes a sure pledge that we shall never cease to be worthy of it. . . . The love of country is in the heart of Jews a sentiment so natural, so powerful, and so consonant to their religious opinions, that a French Jew considers himself in England as among strangers, although he may be among Jews. . . . To such a pitch is this sentiment carried that during the last war, French Jews were seen fighting desperately against other Jews, the subjects of countries at war with France.[5]

Why this passionate commitment to modernity? In the nineteenth century and early twentieth century, many Jews truly believed that the world was on the brink of perfection or, to use the Jewish language, on the verge of the final and total *tikkun*. So much seemed so good. Democracy and civil rights were growing, medical advances were extending both the length and quality of life, and science held out a promise of perfection. Humanity itself was being transformed as people discarded the parochial particularities of religion, town, even family, for a cosmopolitanism that effaced distinctiveness. The Jews believed that they were witnessing an unparalleled convergence of the two great faiths of Christianity and Judaism. In 1888, the German-Jewish philosopher Hermann Cohen stated confidently:

> Our Israelite religion, as it exists in our midst today, has already begun in fact a cultural, historical union with Protestantism. Not only have we more or less definitely and openly thrown off the tradition of the Talmud as binding just as they have discarded the tradition of the Church. But in a much deeper sense, in all the spiritual questions, we think and feel in accord with the Protestant spirit. Thus the common ground in religion is in truth the most powerful and effective unifying force for a genuine national fusion.[6]

This union between liberal Jews and progressive Christians promised a new age of human creativity and freedom. In 1885, for example, the American Reform Movement stated its goals in the Pittsburgh Platform, presenting a clear vision of the revolutionary views of the time:

> We hold that the modern discoveries of scientific researches in the domains of nature and history are not antagonistic to the doctrines of Judaism, the Bible reflecting the primi-

tive ideas of its own age and at times clothing its conception of divine providence and justice dealing with man in
miraculous narratives.

We recognize in the modern era of universal culture of heart
and intellect the approach of the realization of Israel's great
Messianic hope for the establishment of the kingdom of truth,
justice and peace among all men. We consider ourselves no
longer a nation but a religious community, and therefore expect neither a return to Palestine, nor a sacrificial worship
under the administration of the sons of Aaron, nor the resto-
ration of any of the laws concerning the Jewish state.

We recognize in Judaism a progressive religion, ever striving
to be in accord with the postulates of reason. We are convinced of the utmost necessity of preserving the historical
identity with our great past. Christianity and Islam being
daughter-religions of Judaism, we appreciate their mission
to aid in the spreading of monotheistic and moral truth. We
acknowledge that the spirit of broad humanity of our age is
our ally in the fulfillment of our mission, and therefore we
extend the hand of fellowship to all who cooperate with us
in the establishment of the reign of truth and righteousness
among men.[7]

Everything that occurred was seen in terms of this messianic idealism. As traumatic an event as World War I was
called the "war to end all wars," a fulfillment of the prophetic
visions of Isaiah. Marxist ideologies, which today seem so
bankrupt, were viewed by many Jews as a sign of the world's
tikkun, because they promised "to each according to his
ability; to each according to his need."

So powerful was the vision of a united world and so compelling was the Jewish commitment to join the rest of humanity after thousands of years of segregation in the ghetto that
wherever these revolutionary ideas flourished, Jews flocked

to them. For most Jews, getting swept up in these historic events constituted a personal liberation of sorts. They could experiment with unfamiliar foods and fashions, fascinating ideas and new friends. Still, most important was their ability to translate the Jewish call to repair the world into concrete acts, in a world that was finally allowing them to enter.

The modern nation state, some believed, embodied the power to bring all peoples together in a common culture of truth and justice, and a shared destiny of the perfect society. Moritz Lazarus, an esteemed Jewish leader who spoke at the College for the Study of Judaism in Berlin in 1879, imagined a union between Jews and Germany in rapturous prose. To his fellow Jewish leaders and students, he proclaimed:

> My *Volk* are those whom I regard as my *Volk*, whom I call mine, with whom I know myself to be tied by unbreakable bonds. Gentlemen, who are we then? Germans! We are, wish to be, and can be nothing else. Language alone does not make us Germans. The land we inhabit, the state we serve, the law we obey, the scholarship which informs us, the art which inspires us—they are all German. Mother tongue and fatherland are German, both creations of our innermost being. Here stands our cradles; here are the graves of those from whom we descend over many generations. Thus the beginning and the end of our lives is here.[8]

This was not the voice of an assimilationist fleeing his Judaism or the pandering of a frightened little *shtetl* Jew. These words, spoken by a leader of the Jewish community, expressed the vision of a world so informed by the messianic that a failure to grasp the moment and commit to it could only be regarded as heresy.

Step back and examine the basic principles that have been

presented and it is easy to see how smoothly Jews decoded the spiritual message of their traditions and rewrote the script. How better emulate the passion of the prophet who demanded help for the widow, the orphan, and the downtrodden, than by becoming a social revolutionary like Karl Marx? How more purposefully heed Isaiah's cries to lift up the fallen and free the imprisoned than by becoming a lawyer for the poor or a social activist leading demonstrations, as Jews commonly did in Germany, Russia, and the United States? How more radically "open the eyes of the blind" than by helping them to understand their innermost selves, the liberating gift that Sigmund Freud, the father of psychotherapy, offered the world? What more effective way to carry out the lessons of Exodus than by overthrowing dictatorships and corrupt governments, the path of so many young Jews who volunteered for the Abraham Lincoln Brigade, which fought fascism in Spain in the 1930s? Finally, how more lovingly fulfill the Torah's commandment to care for the poor than by using the fruits of financial success to create new social-service agencies and to provide scholarships, as did the Schiffs, Warburgs, Rothschilds, and so many others?

Still, at the end of the nineteenth century and the beginning of the twentieth, Jews remained outsiders struggling to "get in." At this remarkable moment in the history of human progress, the desire to perfect the world most often was synonymous with total integration into the revolutionary forces of change. To remain separate was to abandon the Jewish vision of a world that could be made whole. Yet, paradoxically, that very sense of separateness had preserved the Jewish identity as subverters of absolute ideologies and imperial states. It has been said that Freud (and one could say the same about Einstein, Marx, and many others) *had* to be

Jewish, because revolutionary ideas come from those living outside the conventional norms. Those within the system seldom undermine existing truths or challenge absolute axioms. On his seventieth birthday, Freud (in spite of serious inner conflicts over his Jewish birth) noted:

> Only to my Jewish nature did I owe the two qualities which had become indispensable to me on my hard road. Because I was a Jew I found myself free from many prejudices which limited others in the use of their intellect, and, being a Jew, I was prepared to enter opposition and to renounce agreement with the "compact majority."[9]

The tension between the desire of Jews to be part of the revolution, and the reality, as well as the need for, separateness, was sublimated into a driving determination to be the best Europeans and North Americans possible, the most successful moderns of all.

Tenuous as their newfound status was, the Jews emerging from the ghettoes and *shtetls* slowly were allowed to take part in Western civilization. They seized the opportunity. The newly liberated Jewish community soon provided the best scientists, the most articulate lawyers and jurists, the most creative builders, the sharpest financiers. Otto Preuss authored the German constitution of the Weimar Republic and Walter Rathenau was its most significant minister. Leon Blum was the socialist premier of France. More than half the leading scientists of the Manhattan Project, which created the atomic bomb that ended World War II, were Jews. The government of England could not pay for the Suez Canal, so it took a loan from the Rothschilds. Jews founded or owned the major publishing houses of Germany and the United States, in addition to many of the most influential newspapers in those countries. All the major studios of Hollywood were founded by Jews. The dramatic urban-renewal projects of New York were directed by Robert Moses. Samuel Gompers and Sidney Hillman founded the American Federation of Labor (AFL) and the Congress of Industrial Organizations (CIO), which cared for the needs of workers. Drs. Salk and Sabin discovered vaccines for polio. Nobel Prizes and literary awards, newspapers and theater, medicine, music, and science were captured by Jews who immersed themselves in the Western world with the passion with which they once had studied Talmud.

Were it not for the unparalleled rise in anti-Semitism in Europe that began about 1880 and culminated in the Holocaust, it is possible to imagine that Jews would have been so well integrated into European life that the Jewish people would have ceased to exist. Had the message of Judaism in the modern age truly been universal, had all sensitive and humane people indeed joined together in the name of progress, and had European culture remained as inviting as first imagined, the result surely would have led to a joyous assimilation. In future generations, one would remember an ancestry that was Jewish the way Americans remember that their families came from Scandinavia or Scotland—an interesting fact, but one with no discernible impact on identity or life choices.

Instead, millions of European Jews, among them German Jews who were German in every way and French Jews who were French in every way, were massacred by the Nazis. It is painfully clear that many of these victims, oblivious to any distinction between themselves and their fellow non-Jewish citizens, marched to their deaths with no insight as to why this horror was happening to them. Among those who were murdered were children who had never known that their fathers were born Jews, as well as World War I heroes who had fought bravely in the name of the nation now sending them to the gas chambers. It is ironic that Hitler defined "who is a Jew" in the modern age, uniting the atheist with the believer, the sophisticated Jew and the simple laborer, the Jews of Paris, Berlin, Warsaw, and Saloniki. The Holocaust united its survivors as well, both in guilt over their failure to act on behalf of fellow Jews and in the responsibility they subsequently took upon themselves to battle to save other Jews even as they fight evil in the world.

HOW THE HOLOCAUST FUNDAMENTALLY CHANGED JEWISH THINKING

Judaism and the Jewish people had never confronted such disciplined, absolute, and conscious evil in its entire experience. Here, Irving Greenberg's insights allow us to better understand both the quality of Nazi evil and the inability of Jews to respond to it until the destruction was almost complete. They had imbibed the words of Rabbi Shimon Bar Yohai who lived during the Roman persecutions:

> Precious are chastisements, for their goodly gifts which are coveted by all the nations of the world, were given solely for the sake of their sufferings, and they are: Torah, Eretz Yisrael, and the world to come.[10]

Judaism and the Jewish people, Greenberg maintains, had cultivated an ethic of powerlessness as its crucial metaphor and secret source of sacredness. The countless persecutions and humiliations of Jewish Diaspora life could be given meaning through this ethic of powerlessness. Each increment of suffering was seen as an expression of God's will, a form of chastisement that promised ever greater divine love. Even the highly secularized Jews of Germany responded to the anti-Semitic outbursts of the 1870s in this traditional fashion. In a public statement, the Board of Co-religionists (the euphemism for Judaism used by Jews at that time) ended by explaining "how a Jew is to handle himself" in light of the violent attacks: "Above all, let Jews see in their present pain a touch of Providence guiding them toward self-improvement."[11] Little could those who believed this imagine that the final solution would not be Providential chastisement, but total genocide.

Greenberg explains that for eighteen hundred years rabbis responded to the expulsions, defamations, and assaults by validating their pariah status. While all the evidence showed Judaism to be on the fringes of humanity, the rabbis insisted that, in truth, it was at the center of the world, for the entire universe was sustained through Jewish spiritual steadfastness in observing the commandments. Christian or Muslim power would prove ephemeral, they were sure, while Jewish values would triumph. Suffering only elevated the value of the Jews in God's eyes.[12]

The ethic of powerlessness grew stronger as Jews were banished further from the dominant society and from the politics and concerns that preoccupied the non-Jewish world. In fact, the forced segregation in the premodern period only increased the Jews' willing retreat from the gentile domain. Powerlessness became a way to assert moral power and superiority. Clear distinctions were made between Jewish and gentile character and behavior: While gentiles filled the world with murder, rape, and decadence, Jews strove to do God's will. The gentile took pleasure in sports (*goyische naches*) while Jews found joy in the study of Torah. In one extreme of this dichotomy, gentile souls were animal-like, while Jewish souls were Godlike. The obvious conclusion: a vibrant Jewish life only needed internal autonomy and solidarity; that is, the more removed from their surroundings, the better. Let the gentiles have their kings, it was agreed, while Jews governed their own inner world. As the rabbi in *Fiddler on the Roof* exclaims: "May God keep the Czar far, far away from us."

This world view, which raised powerlessness to a moral virtue, protected Jews from physical and political realities that might otherwise have been overwhelming. They could intensely debate the prerogatives of Jewish kings and imagine a rebuilt Temple in Jerusalem, even as they were being expelled from their homes and countries. The outer world might brutalize them, but they knew that the ultimate victory was theirs.

Nothing, however, prepared Jews and Judaism for the Nazis, who had dedicated themselves to the total destruction of both. Nazism rose in the citadel of modernity, in the midst of its ideals of goodness and justice. In fact, the Nazis perverted those very ideals to provide a rationale for their own agenda. Like the moderns, the Germans foresaw an imminent redemption. They read in Hitler's vision the final stage of "world perfection." Harnessing the most advanced forms of technology, the peerless German bureaucracy applied itself ceaselessly to the task of "world perfection" by systematically and dispassionately murdering Jews and all others whom they imagined stood between reality and the realization of their ideal. The universalistic principles of modernity were perversely applied as well: no Jew was exempt from the Nazi decrees; all were equal, irrespective of status, talent, or commitment to Judaism—proof that irrational and petty hatreds had been overcome.[13]

If Jews had from the beginning of their history represented a life force, with a mission to prod others to perfect the world, then Hitler was the death force, determined to defeat life itself. Hitler understood the Jewish message perfectly, as well as its corollary: as long as one Jew was alive, the absoluteness of the Nazi truths would be impossible to sustain. By their mere existence, Jews denied Hitler's perfect system. Only they stood between the defeats of the past and the triumph he craved.

As one whose family was gassed and shot throughout Europe during World War II, I have spent my life seeking meaning from the Nazi destruction. In my search for answers, I discovered Primo Levi, an Italian scientist who wrote about his experiences in Auschwitz. What drew me to Levi was the paradox of his passion for life in the death camp, where he clung to each breath in order to survive and tell the story, and his suicide in 1987.

Primo Levi describes the systematic degradation employed by the Nazis, which changed him from human being to *Musselman,* a subhuman, almost lifeless entity with a shriveled soul. In a passage from *Survival at Auschwitz* that describes the execution of one of the few prisoners in the camp who tried to rebel, Levi captures the dehumanization of the Jews witnessing the event:

> Everyone heard the cry of the doomed man, it pierced through the old thick barriers of inertia and submissiveness, it struck the living core of man in each of us: *"Kamaraden, ich bin der Letze!"* ("Comrades, I am the last one!")
> I wish I could say that from the midst of us, an abject flock,

a voice rose, a murmur, a sign of assent. But nothing happened. We remained standing, bent and grey, our heads dropped, and we did not uncover our heads until the German ordered us to do so. The trap door opened, the body wriggled horribly; the (Jewish) band began playing again and we were once more lined up and filed past the quivering body of the dying man.

At the foot of the gallows, the SS watch us pass with indifferent eyes: their work is finished, and well finished. The Russians can come now: there are no longer any strong men among us. . . . The Russians can come now: they will only find us, the slaves, the worn-out, worthy of the unarmed death that awaits us.[14]

The dehumanization accomplished by the Nazis was accompanied by the destruction of the sustaining faith that Jews had carried with them for almost two thousand years: that their suffering was their salvation, a means of self-improvement to hasten the coming of the messiah. The Holocaust invalidated that faith, because there could be no redemption in total extermination. Levi writes of old Kuhn, praying and crying aloud, swaying back and forth in a song of thanksgiving for being saved from the gas chambers on a particular day's selection, and he wonders: Does not Kuhn recognize that his momentary salvation, at the cost of the lives of so many others, is an abomination "which no propitiatory prayer, no pardon, no expiation by the guilty, which nothing in the power of man can ever clean again"? Levi concludes: "If I were God, I would spit at Kuhn's prayer."[15]

The Holocaust was a direct assault on the Jewish vision of a world moving to perfection. It mocked Judaism's contention that each human life is of infinite worth. Throughout the war, Nazi technology sought to reduce the cost of mass extermination. By the end, Irving Greenberg writes, babies were being thrown into the gas chambers over the heads of the adult bodies crammed in there while the quantity of gas used was decreased. This prolonged the agony of choking, but the reduction in gas in addition to the extra bodies killed, saved the Nazis two-fifths of one cent per Jewish death. So little was a Jewish life worth.[16]

The Torah maintains that life is ever-increasing in richness and diversity, but the Nazis' particular violence against children and pregnant women seemed to make a lie of that belief, as well. One third of the Jews murdered by the Nazis were children; pregnant women or mothers with infants were condemned to immediate gassing. The breasts of nursing mothers were taped so that they and all the *Musselmen* could watch life wither and die—the annihilation of the soul as well as the body.

THE PROBLEM OF MEANING AFTER THE HOLOCAUST

But the greatest triumph of Nazism was the attack of the "Final Solution" on the very idea of a universe that has meaning. George Orwell aptly described a totalitarian world in which the very meaninglessness of evil becomes the ultimate horror:

> You must stop imagining that posterity will vindicate you, Winston. Posterity will never hear of you. You will be lifted clean out from the stream of history. We shall turn you into gas and pour you into the stratosphere. Nothing will remain of you: not a name in a register, not a memory in a living brain. You will be annihilated in the past as well as in the future. You will never have existed. . . . We shall squeeze you empty, and then fill you with ourselves.[17]

These words of the interrogator, written in the era of Nazism
and Stalinism, still chill to the bone. Winston is being taught
that human existence has no intrinsic or coherent meaning
at all. It is the terror haunting us deep inside: that one's existence means nothing at all.

Diabolical as the Nazi machine was, it had competition from
the Soviet state. The Communist regime also presented a perfect vision and higher truth. With new powers derived from
scientific advances, the totalitarian Marxist governments consciously contrived to eradicate all human rights and to strip
away each person's uniqueness and dignity. The only truth
was that proclaimed by the state. Children were trained to
denounce their parents, those denounced were brutalized until
they publicly admitted to heresies and treason. Artists were
told what to paint and composers what music to score. Writers could only mimic what the state sanctioned. Every facet
of life was controlled. Since the government expressed the will
of the people, a person who disagreed with the government
was, by definition, a sociopath. To protect the perfect vision
the state represented, a dissenter had to be hospitalized, isolated, tortured, or murdered. Far more brutal than the inquisitions once instituted by the Church in the name of God, the
Communist show trials and absolutist policies condemned to
death millions in the name of the Marxist state.

As with Nazism, the very existence of Jews posed a fatal
challenge to the absolute truths of the Soviets. Every aspect
of Jewish identity thus was suppressed—even the right of
Jewish Communists to train and mobilize other Jews to be
good Marxists. Jewish writers and organizers were murdered.
Yiddish, the national language of East European Jewry, was
outlawed.

In a century that began with the flowering of freedoms and
the triumph of humanism, no one could have predicted this

life-and-death battle for the soul of the world and the nadir to which humanity would sink. For those of us too young to have lived through the nightmare, it is difficult to conceive that such evil really existed. Today, one sees only caricatures of Hitler or Stalin. But for the Jews (and others) who had taken up as their mission the struggle for human freedom over repression and fear, this was a fight to the death. And death seemed to win. The stench of the death camps and gulags, the images of mass graves and stacked corpses became so much a part of our vision of modernity that a reasonable person, not to mention a rational people, would abandon all notions of human dignity and crawl away in defeat.

Primo Levi writes in 1958, as if anticipating his own inability to bear the remembered grief:

> You who live safe
> In your warm houses
> You who find, returning in the evening,
> Hot food and friendly faces:
> Consider if this is a man
> Who works in the mud
> Who does not know peace
> Who fights for a scrap of bread
> Who dies because of a yes or a no.
> Consider if this is a woman
> With no more strength to remember,
> Her eyes empty and her womb cold
> Like a frog in winter.
> Meditate that this came about:
> I commend these words to you.
> Carve them in your hearts
> At home, in the street,
> Going to bed, rising;
> Repeat them to your children,

Or may your house fall apart,
May illness impede you,
May your children turn their faces from you.[18]

CHOOSING LIFE AFTER THE HOLOCAUST

Despite all the evidence, however, Jews chose life—again. Bereft of the traditional theological certainties that had guided and supported them through the dark days of exile, shorn of their optimistic faith in the humanistic powers of modernity, they yet chose life. Automatically, intuitively, they affirmed the vision that had been nurtured for millennia. However, what once was commanded by the force of an omniscient God now was the free-will choice of the Jewish people. Irving Greenberg articulates this profound insight:

> What then happened to the covenant? I submit that its authority was broken, but the Jewish people, released from its obligations, chose voluntarily to take it on again. We are living in the age of the renewal of the covenant. God was no longer in a position to command, but the Jewish people was so in love with the dream of redemption that it volunteered to carry on its mission.[19]

On the simplest and most primitive level, Jews affirmed their early faith by renewing the covenant with new life. My sister was born even as our family was being decimated. Her middle name is Joy. My brother was named Shalom (peace). The synagogue my family helped found was named Temple Ezra, after the leader of the remnant of the Jewish people who returned to Jerusalem following the destruction of the First Temple. By 1945, more Jews were born—in camps and on boats, in villages and cities, leading to the first natural rise in the Jewish population of the West since the turn of the century. Groups of Jews gathered, rebuilt the old and established new communities throughout the world. In the face of the greatest assault in their history and in the absence of any visible response from God to the rupture of the covenantal promise of a partnership dedicated to heal the world, Jews emulated the God they *remembered* by creating new life from the lifelessness of Nazism. They affirmed that the world still could be redeemed.

For the Jews alive in 1948 who had witnessed the Holocaust, no event in Jewish history equaled the successful battle for Jewish independence in *Eretz Yisrael*. The establishment of the State of Israel only three years after the liberation of Jews from the last death camps is no coincidence. The magnitude of Hitler's evil cried for a commensurate affirmation of life—nothing less than the recreation of the vision of Jewish freedom that had died two thousand years earlier. If the Holocaust showed the Jewish people in its most abject powerlessness, then the reestablishment of the State of Israel signified the Jewish people's return to power and their reentry into history as a whole nation. Chaim Weizmann, a founding father of the State of Israel, declared before the 1946 Anglo-American Commission of Inquiry:

> I do not know how many Einsteins, how many Freuds, have been destroyed in the furnaces of Auschwitz and Maidenaek. But there is one thing I know; if we can prevent it, it will never happen again.[20]

To understand Jews and the Jewish people today demands recognition of the revolutionary magnitude of these two events, for the generation of Jews living in the shadow of the

Holocaust and the glow of Israel's rebirth has been irrevocably transformed.

North American Christians or urbane European cosmopolitans of goodwill who like to view the materialism of property, politics, and national borders as a diminution of the spiritual message of religion and universal ethics, must understand that neither dialogue with nor understanding of Jews are possible without confronting the linkage between the Holocaust and the State of Israel. To a people denied the fundamental right to breathe by a world that willingly watched its destruction, the State of Israel gives dignity and self-worth, even as it upholds the uniqueness of the Jewish people. Jews may condemn the policies of the government of Israel with vitriolic critiques, lambasting right or left. But underlying the debate is the steely resolve and undeniable celebration of the Jewish assumption of autonomy and power as a most fitting response to Nazism and, for that matter, Communism as well. Irwin Kula elaborates:

> I am convinced this is why Israel is so significant in contemporary Jewish identity and why trips and missions to Israel generate support for Israel, in a myriad of forms that seem to have the status of *mitzvah*. In some fundamental way, after nineteen hundred years of being told that our exile and wandering were the result of divine rejection—that our weakness and suffering were because of our sins—the return to the land has reaffirmed the deeper intuition that our people's role in history will never be rejected by God no matter what. That we are still beloved of God . . . God's children. . . . This sense of being unconditionally accepted/loved is given legal expression in [Israel's] law of return. All Jews are welcome: worthy, unworthy, good, bad, connected, disconnected. This is the ground on which

demands make sense and why so many feel a sense of *mitzvah* towards Israel.[21]

Eichmann proclaimed that, even if caught, "I will leap into my grave laughing," out of a certainty that the Jewish people, having been reduced in value to mere pennies, would never recover from the blow. The most significant Jewish answer to that assumption is the State of Israel's commitment to gathering in Jews from the four corners of the earth. This is more than the understandable enterprise of the renewed Jewish state. Supported by an extraordinary infrastructure of fund-raising, missions to Israel, and a willingness to fight all those who would challenge the safety of the State of Israel, Jews around the world have paid billions of dollars to save Jewish lives where, only a few decades earlier, the life of a Jew was not even worth two-fifths of one cent. No image better captures the reaffirmation in life and redemption than the unified effort of a people, one generation removed from genocide, to bring home its brothers and sisters "on eagles' wings" to *Eretz Yisrael*.

Jews have chosen voluntarily to renew the covenant and, in so doing, to choose life. But, though they remain committed to the idealistic goals of modernism, something has irrevocably changed. No longer can the means to support the covenant and promote healing in the world be located in the same modernity that nurtured Nazism and Stalinism. True, Jewish modernity cannot deny its intimate and valuable links with Western civilization and, in particular, North American culture. But the conscious covenantal affirmation of Jews today demands that they draw from their Jewish past to construct a new world of meaning as they restore the unique Jewish mission to repair the world.[22]

8

Shattering the Idolatrous: Seeking Sacredness

We come to the late twentieth century, our own time. What can be the meaning of the *brit* to those Jews who live in North America, a world of multiple choices and few obligations? Here are the Jews, nurtured in a tradition that tells them: Each human being is created in the divine image; Jews were liberated to be subversive, to undermine the present in order to improve the future; it is your responsibility to heal a world that is hemorrhaging. And here is Western democracy, whose strongest ethic seems to be the rejection of any diminution of personal freedom and autonomy. The challenge for the conscious Jew is to balance the values and presumptions of a secular, democratic world with the Jewish mission. And in so doing, imagine new and vital ways to continue the story.

The Method of Sacredness

This responsibility is now being played out in North America, an open and accepting democracy which cultivates a world of choices. There are very few forces that push Jews toward covenantal commitment. American society is compelling: comfortable, future-oriented, nonauthoritarian. It frees its citizens to dream of becoming whatever they can imagine and demands few obligations in return. A citizen must pay taxes and abide by the laws of the land. The more motivated may vote in elections or join community organizations to advance certain social or political goals. But here one *voluntarily* accepts or rejects a civic or religious role. Nothing is compelled. In fact, any attempt by the government to control the choices of its citizens—be it by drafting young men into military service, limiting the right to smoke, or prohibiting the purchase of guns—provokes immediate outcries. The great virtue of America is the right of its citizens to choose or not choose their own version of "life, liberty and the pursuit of happiness."

Judaism counters with a command: Choose life. The choice has unique implications. As the human partner in the covenant, the Jew personally accepts a mission of perfecting the world and the obligation to seek a life filled with a sense of sacredness. The task is to discover how one seeks sacredness in the age in which he or she lives.[1]

We have discussed the mission of *tikkun* as perceived by Jews over time and explored some of the traditions of the Jewish people. But what it means to experience one's own life as sacred, or *kadosh*, has only been intimated. The Torah and all later Jewish texts are permeated with the word and its derivations. The prayer recited over wine is called the *kiddush*. The Aramaic words intoned in memory of one who has died is the *kaddish*. Many blessings use the phrase *asher kiddeshanu*—blessed is God who has made us sacred. *Kid-*

dushin is the name given to the Jewish wedding ceremony in which husband and wife commit themselves to each other. The *mikdash* is the Jerusalem Temple where sacrifices were offered to God. All these words derive from the same Hebrew root (*k-d-sh*) whose meaning, at the heart of Judaism, establishes another foundational pillar of Judaism.

Early in the experience of the Jewish people, the word *kadosh* held some frightening implications. Danger surrounded those things that were termed as *kadosh*:

> Now Aaron's sons Nadav and Avihu each took his fire pan, laid fire and incense in it, and offered alien fire before the Lord which [God] had not commanded. And fire erupted from the Lord and consumed them. . . . Then Moses said to Aaron, "This is what the Lord meant in saying: Through those near to Me I will be made *kadosh*, and gain glory before all the people." (Leviticus 10:1-3)

In a rebellion against Moses and Aaron, some of the rebels offered incense and were consumed with fire. Then the Lord ordered Eleazer, the senior son of the High Priest, to

> remove the fire pans—for they have become *kadosh*—from among the burnt remains; scatter the coals around. . . . Make them into hammered sheets to plate the altar, for once they have been used as an offering to the Lord, they have become *kadosh*. (Numbers 17:1-3)

That which was designated as *kadosh* apparently exuded a physical force that was transferred like an electrical current. As with electricity, if something *kadosh* was touched incorrectly, it could kill.

However, the word *kadosh* means something more than danger, for how else explain these verses from the book of Leviticus:

> The Lord spoke to Moses saying: Speak to the whole Israel-
> ite community and say to them: "You shall be *kadosh*, for I
> the Lord your God, am *kadosh*." (Leviticus 19:1)

In this context, *kadosh* also designates that which is special, set aside or to be used only under set circumstances. The specific actions of the priests, particular foods to be eaten, sacred places to be approached—all required that the rules of *kedushah* be followed. An animal, once designated *kadosh* for sacrifice, could never be used for some other purpose, even if it turned out that the animal was defective and could not be offered on the altar.

But *kadosh* refers to more than priestly functions or certain places and objects. God is *kadosh*, and Jews are directed to be like God, to be *kadosh*. Returning to the book of Genesis reminds us that human beings are so significant and filled with potential that the Torah says they are created in God's image. Later in the Torah, we are told that those bound to the covenant at Sinai can make their lives sacred. Obviously the potential for sacredness is linked with the Jewish path toward *tikkun*. *Kedushah* provides a new range of meanings by which to understand human action.

In the verse from Leviticus cited above, all Israelites are instructed to make their lives *kadosh*: women and men, children and the elderly, every class of profession and status. In these words resonate the echo of God's pledge at Mount Sinai: "You shall be a kingdom of priests and a people who is *kadosh*" (Exodus 19:6). There is a democratic distinctiveness about these texts, especially striking for an ancient community. Even in the new United States, only landed Caucasian males were free and had the right (expected, but not obligated) to mold the nation through their vote and other forms of political participation befitting gentlemen. In many religious communities, there is a designated religious elite; the saint separates himself or herself from the rest of the community, living an ascetic life of purity. In the Torah, *all* members of the society are commanded (and obligated) to be Godlike through the ways they live their everyday lives. The potential for *kedushah* is universal.

In the religious traditions of the West, sacredness is a feeling. In Christianity, sacredness is achieved through a spiritual encounter, an awareness visited upon a person through an experience of the divine. One imagines a painting with angels and halos, a beatific visage with head tilted toward heaven. In Eastern religions, sacredness is found in a sense of oneness which can be achieved despite the material and physical world that impinges on the soul. Pain and suffering are to be conquered by focus and meditation. There are Jewish traditions that incorporate these approaches as well, and for many generations when Jews felt powerless to effect change in the world, such passivity in the face of life's bitter conditions was the norm. Today, one still finds strains within the Jewish people who believe that one should not force God's hand, that the task of human beings is to be obedient and passive in the face of suffering. And in response to the failures of modernity to deliver all it seemed to promise, Jewish prayer, meditation, and other eclectic signs of spiritual rebirth are growing. But such views, even today, are not dominant. *Kedushah* remains grounded in this world.

Judaism views sacredness as a process that moves from

the commonplace to the unique and Godlike. Common does not mean profane or evil. Rather, it refers to what is normal, regular, expected. Common describes the world of aphorisms that permeate our culture: Strive for success, get more of the action, make it through the day, do what needs to be done. In that world, a person plays by the rules set by the school or job, home or government. Common is the culture in which Americans live much of their lives, shopping at malls and going out to fast-food joints, looking for a bargain and a place to spend free time. There is nothing wicked about common-ness, but its product is complacency. The common life brings with it a banal contentment rather than any consciousness of the fate of the universe or one's role in changing it. A strik-ing aspect of the American Jewish psyche is the need to be just like everyone else, to be common.

Sex, food, money, property—these are the basics of human existence. Everybody wants them. In American culture, where more is always better, honor often goes to those who have more sex, food, money, and property. What one chooses to do with the sex, food, money, and property acquired is pretty much up to the individual. Again, Judaism differs: A person is directed to achieve *kedushah* and *kedushah* demands that one strive for different goals. A few examples will strike the contrast.

The earth was given to human beings, the psalmist pro-claims, so humans are commanded to master it and utilize its resources. Yet clear title and ownership of property as sanctified in British and American traditions is not sanctioned in biblical law. Rather, the Torah teaches that human beings are custodians of a divine trust:

> When you enter the land and plant any tree for food, you shall consider its fruit as forbidden. For three years it is forbidden

to you and is not to be eaten. In the fourth year all its fruit shall be set aside for jubilation before the Lord and only in the fifth year can you use its fruit. (Leviticus 19:23-25)

Much of the material acquisitions of life may be consumed, yet Jews are obligated to tithe their earnings to God—that is, to provide for the needs of others.

When you reap the harvest of your land, you shall not reap all the way to the edge of your field, or gather the gleanings from your harvest. You shall not pick your vineyard bare, or gather the fallen fruit of your vineyard. You shall leave them for the poor and the stranger: I am the Lord your God. (Leviticus 19:9-10)

Human beings must eat, but the Torah instructs Jews to be *kadosh* through limiting the animals that they eat.

For I am the Lord, the One who brought you up from the land of Egypt to be your God: you shall be *kadosh*, for I am *kadosh*. These are the instructions concerning animals, birds, all living creatures that move in the water, and all creatures that swarm on the earth, for distinguishing between the impure and the pure, between the living things that may be eaten and the living things that may not be eaten. (Leviticus 11:45-47)

Kedushah is the process whereby human beings make the common components of their lives more Godlike. Martin Buber elaborates: "For there is no rung of being on which we cannot find the holiness (*kedushah*) of God everywhere and at all times."[2]

Kedushah, focusing as it does on common, everyday action that can be raised to the Godlike, is neither esoteric nor mysterious. It does not associate holiness with special feelings or experiences available only to people who are mystical or dedicated enough to locate it. *Kedushah* is always available and to everybody. Not only Jews have had this insight, although for three millennia Jews have been preoccupied with expanding the territory of *kedushah*. In "Aurora Leigh," a poetic reading of Moses' encounter with God at the Burning Bush, the Victorian poet Elizabeth Barrett Browning wrote:

> Earth is crammed with heaven
> And every common bush afire with God.
> Only those who see take off their shoes
> The rest sit 'round and pluck blackberries

Pablo Casals, in his autobiography, also exulted in those moments when the commonplace became transcendent:

> For the past eighty years, I have started each day in the same manner. It is not a mechanical routine but something essential to my daily life. I go to the piano, and I play two preludes and fugues of Bach. I cannot think of doing otherwise. It is a sort of benediction on the house. But that is not its only meaning for me. It is a rediscovery of the world which I have the joy of being a part. It fills me with awareness of the wonder of life, with a feeling of the incredible marvel of being a human being. The music is never the same for me, never. Each day it is something new, fantastic and unbelievable.[3]

Human beings are distinct from other forms of life in that they spend their lives seeking meaning. It is remarkable how, in spite of the struggle just to survive, cultures, families, and individuals are often preoccupied with elevating even the most simple acts to a higher level of meaning through rituals and stories, music and art. Next time you take a walk, think about the effort and imagination people have expended to construct a house and tend a garden. Consider the creative energy that goes into writing a play or an article, into making something beautiful. The world is filled with the traces of our inner lives, as well as those of people long gone, who put uniquely personal imprints on seemingly random experience and transmitted what they learned and experienced to the next generation. Religious cultures, and their traditions, attempt to provide a framework of meaning in a seemingly chaotic universe.

The traditions Judaism developed imagine a world in which each and every action has the potential for *kedushah*— if only people look. Each action or obligation is called a *mitzvah*. Doing a *mitzvah* is the key that allows each person to tap into *kedushah* and to experience the sacred. The rabbis provided the simple formula of a blessing to mark the observance of an act of *kedushah*:

> Blessed are You, Source of the Universe, who has made us *kadosh* through the *mitzvot*, and obligates us . . .

The sages who constructed these blessings some two thousand years ago saw them as a way to focus a person's attention on the miracles of existence. Not to do so, in the view of some Torah scholars, would be a kind of spurning of gifts:

> Our Rabbis have taught: It is forbidden to enjoy anything of this world without a blessing, and if anyone enjoys anything of this world without a blessing, that person commits a sacrilege.[4]

The obligations required by the system of *mitzvot* are myriad, from kindling candles at sundown to illumine the Sabbath to eating *matzah* on Passover as a reminder of liberation, from washing hands in the manner of the priests to engaging in study. *Mitzvah* is the way to elevate the common to the sacred, making life something new, fantastic and unbelievable. *Mitzvah* is also the human part of renewing the covenantal relationship with God.

Nothing is too mundane to be elevated by and seen as a blessing. Even the most basic biological functions, such as digesting and eliminating food, demand that a person stop and reflect on the significance of the human body and the wonder of being alive:

> Blessed are You, Source of the Universe, who with wisdom created human beings and provided each with tubes and vessels. It is known and revealed before You that if even one opens or closes at the wrong moment, we could not remain alive and stand before You. Blessed are You, Healer of all life and Creator of wonders.[5]

The Holiness of Commitment

The link between a *mitzvah* and *kedushah* means that any action is potentially sacred. This is best expressed in a strange hierarchy of values discussed by the Rabbis:

> Greater is one who is commanded and fulfills the obligation than one who is not commanded yet [voluntarily] fulfills the obligation.[6]

For most of us, this is exactly backwards. Certainly, the person who has no responsibility to do something good but does it voluntarily should be superior to the person who feels coerced into compliance with the law. Why credit the recalcitrant one who is dragged into fulfilling a *mitzvah*? But a subtle psychological insight and sensitivity informs the Jewish approach to the sacred. Two typical examples will serve to illustrate:

A young single woman walks through a park and sees two children, a brother and sister, fighting. She kneels down and sweetly separates the children, resolving their conflict with a few words. Undoubtedly, it is a virtuous act, a good deed. The same two children then return home, where an older brother is cramming for a college exam. Actually, he has just taken a break to repair a leaking faucet and is now throwing some leftovers together for dinner with his siblings. Exhausted from a grueling week of study, he hears the two fighting—for the fifth time that day. He tries to ignore the screaming, feels his temper rising. Instead of exploding, however, he takes a deep breath, kneels down (not so sweetly) to separate the kids, resolving their conflict with a few words.

A man and woman meet at a dance. They are attracted to each other and, after a romantic evening, decide that they want to make love. They return to the woman's apartment and spend a passionate night pleasing each other. In the morning, although the excitement of the sexual experience remains, each realizes that this was a one-time affair. They separate, never to see each other again, but with a feeling of sexual satisfaction. Elsewhere, a couple that has been married for twenty years returns home from work late. After rushing to make dinner, help the kids through their homework, straighten up the house (there was no time in the morning), and pay the bills, they finally settle into bed at eleven o'clock. The husband realizes that his wife wants to be caressed and cared for after a long day; she senses that he would love to be sexually excited. Energy is low and they are too tired to make love, but they spend a small amount of time with a quick massage before going to sleep. They wake up in each other's arms, looking forward to their next vacation when they will have the luxury of some time together.

The contrasting scenes in these examples can shed light on what the Rabbis so valued in the person who lives with a sense of relationship that commands obligation. The voluntary actions of the young woman in the park are virtuous but undependable. The one-night lovers act so very naturally, like the beautiful carefree people that inhabit commercials. Certainly, television or movies never portray tired married couples making love (if they do, sex is invariably interrupted by a crying child or a telephone call). But the brother and the married couple in the situations above act out of a deep sense of relationship and obligation, which is what the Rabbis valued so highly. Their behaviors are covenantal, motivated by love and long-term commitment—a sparse commodity in our age of divorce and family break-ups. In these two scenes, the brother and the married couple perform a *mitzvah*.

Sacredness is not merely a product of a particular activity at a particular moment, but the willingness to commit one's whole life to a web of relationships, obligations, and purpose. By valuing commitment over whim or passion alone, Judaism learned to regard the person who accepts ongoing responsibility as the greater hero and role model. Sometimes a *mitzvah* is done poorly or without great meaning. One may sometimes cut corners or even ignore an obligation. But because any one action is part of a larger scheme, a response to hearing and accepting the covenantal relationship at Sinai, the intent is to elevate a range of life's common behaviors to the sacred. Abraham Joshua Heschel writes of the grandeur in this commitment:

> Of one thing, however, I am sure. There is a challenge that I can never evade, in moments of failure as in moments of achievement. Man is inescapably, essentially challenged on all levels of his existence. It is in his being challenged that he discovers himself as a human being. Do I exist as a human being? My answer is: *I am commanded—therefore I am.* There is a built-in *sense of indebtedness in the consciousness of man,* an awareness of *owing gratitude,* of being *called upon* at certain moments to reciprocate, to answer, to live in a way which is compatible with the grandeur and mystery of living.[7]

CAN JUDAISM COMPETE IN THE FREE MARKET OF IDEAS?

As discussed in the previous chapter, the covenantal relationship between God and human beings is transforming even as the circumstances of the Jewish people are transforming since the Holocaust and the establishment of the State of Israel. Rather than obedience, it is now predicated on the choice of Jews to take on commitments voluntarily. This, of necessity, has also changed the attitude of Jews toward the traditions they have inherited. For many years, when Jews lived as an independent nation in *Eretz Yisrael* and later, within autonomous communities, Jewish law was made and elaborated by religious leaders. The people were obligated to follow it. Much of the Torah, the Talmud, and the various codes of the medieval period were based on that assumption, providing prohibitions as well as punishments for in-fractions of the law. Though Jewish law cannot be enforced in North America today, most Jews still think of Judaism as a series of rules.

If Judaism is a legal system with borders and high walls separating that which is permitted from that which is for-bidden, then the task of its leaders would be to further codify who is in and who is out, which behavior is sanctioned and which is not. The challenge would be only whether or not to obey the law. Judaism would involve little personal struggle for meaning, but would demand learning the obligations of the law. For those who adhere to Judaism as a divinely con-structed code of law, it is both comforting and meaningful to be part of that system and the community it fosters, and to feel confident in the role of servant to God. In this case, *kedushah* is found in obedience, in doing God's will as com-manded by the rabbis in the traditional legal codes. On the other hand, for those who refuse to accept Jewish traditions as commands, it is easy to say: "Since I am on the other side, I have no obligation to follow any laws." But neither of these approaches seems adequate or responsive to this age of in-comprehensible losses and remarkable power, affluence, and freedom. Judaism is more than its legal system and attendant traditions, compelling and valuable as they may be.

And, indeed, for many Jews today, neither the approach of single-minded adherence to laws nor that of complete ab-dication of the responsibility to observe such laws is a satis-fying response to their need for meaning and commitment. The freedom and openness of American society, decried by ethnic minorities and religious communities as the source of their demise, can, in fact, be a great asset to Jewish survival. If Judaism and all other movements that offer alternatives to the dominant culture will succeed, they will do so in an open market of values, ideas, and competitive traditions. No longer are minorities in North America (except, painfully, those of color) forced into a certain identity. The fear of assimilation is the result of a deeper insecurity that Judaism cannot compel adherence by virtue of its ideas and compete within a democratic framework.

The challenge for Jews in the United States and Canada is to experience commitment—a sense of *mitzvah*—within a wholly voluntary setting. The most strictly observant Jewish teenager, one who has sidelock *peyot* and wears a hat and a long black coat, is free to change into blue jeans and a T-shirt, walk out of the Jewish community and never return. No court in North America will force a Jew to observe the Sabbath and no jail will incarcerate a person for adultery. If Judaism is to retain its power over its adherents and persuade them to accept human responsibility, then it is necessary to utilize a new model.

In the new paradigm, Jewish "law" is presented neither as Jews in prior centuries understood it nor in terms of its common secular meaning. Instead, every *mitzvah* is seen as a significant decision to be made by an individual. There are no human courts any longer to judge such decisions of personal commitment and meaning. In the imagery of the sages, each person must stand before God, who will judge whether his or her decisions were right or wrong. Yet the traditions Jews have inherited are abandoned at great risk, for Jewish life is a web of interconnected *mitzvot* and relationships. Each person is asked to hear and heed the challenge to choose life and become part of the enterprise of repairing the world.

REACHING TOWARD KEDUSHAH

It may help to imagine God (unknowable, yet in Jewish tradition, the ultimate in *kedushah*) at the center of the universe, pulling at thoughts and behaviors like a magnet. The *mitzvot* of Judaism, the blessings recited, the rituals that fill the Jewish day, week, and year, all are vehicles to elevate common human behaviors to a higher state of consciousness and bring them closer to the magnet at the center. The more an individual and the community of which he or she is a part act out of commitment and values that reflect *kedushah*, the closer their orbit around the sacred magnetic core. Some people, well supported by family and friends, naturally rotate closer to the core. There are those who search alone to find their place within the covenant. Others may feel less attracted to the pull of the magnet and it may be hard for them, and for their fellow Jews, to view their behaviors as Jewish; they may be rotating in an outer orbit. And in some cases, behaviors will be so far from the central core of *kedushah* that there will be no pull at all. Those individuals and communities will no longer be part of the Jewish universe and will spin away. This is not a mechanical process, decided by a board of rabbis or judicial fiat. Building a Jewish world of *kedushah* in this age is an evolutionary process. At any given moment, one cannot predict who is beyond the magnetic pull and who still is within the orbit of *kedushah*.

And no person consistently stays within one orbit. Human beings are complex; their motivations are mixed, their behaviors are never entirely positive or negative. Some actions may pull an individual closer to the core, while others may push her to the outer limits. Each time a person circles around, he may fantasize that he is coming closer, though anger, pain, frustration, or exhaustion may drag him back outward. This sense of circling around is a good Jewish image. Like Passover and the Day of Atonement, Yom Kippur, or reading the Torah, it contains the idea of return. One has been there before, eating the *matzah* and lighting the candles. The story of Isaac's birth or crossing the sea was read in the synagogue last year, as it will be the next. So it is in life. Issues and memories seemingly long resolved reappear, forcing a person to address them once again. Living as a Jew is an activist's lifetime endeavor.

In these ways, too, Jews can experience the cyclical nature of life: birth, growth, procreation, death. Yet, as has been shown, from the first chapter of Genesis to the Exodus from Egypt, the Torah does not see human beings locked into an ever-repeating pattern. Each person is created in God's image, filled with infinite potential, expected to grow and change. Nor is the world frozen. The universe is evolving, life forms growing ever more complex. And human beings can be partners in the triumph of life over death. But even as human growth must be measured in small increments, so the world changes only step by step. Though the process may seem painfully gradual, to believe this is to assert that the orbits of one's life need not be a repetitive circle. Instead, imagine a spiral where the curves are never quite the same. The more one makes his or her life *kadosh*, the closer one spirals to the central Godliness. The more a Jewish community experiences *mitzvah* as the obligation which emerges from relationship, the better partner it will be to the divine.

The challenge of *kedushah* starts at the individual level. Judaism's position is: Possibly, at this moment, you do not have the capacity to perfect everything. In that case, start with an aspect of yourself. The expectation, however, is always that one will move beyond the self, because personal perfection is not sufficient unless the world is healed as well. That, too, should be the proper focus of one's energies. The personal sense of mission is reinforced by families and friends who join together in a community that strives to fulfill the covenantal obligation of repairing the world. This explains why the mystical rabbis who lived in Tzefat believed that Jews could bring the world to a final redemptive *tikkun*: Imagine if every Jew would commit his and her life to the mission of liberation by subverting the self-satisfied institutions and political systems. Would the perfect world be far behind?

9

GOD'S JUSTICE: DOING *TZEDAKAH*

Our times are preoccupied with the existence and needs of the autonomous self. And, indeed, Judaism begins with a single individual raising the commonplace to the sacred in his or her own life. Yet the traditions that contemporary Jews inherited direct them to construct a just society in which individuals are required to participate in repairing the world by upgrading the quality of life for those around them. This is not a fiction piously pronounced, but the obligation of a covenantal community. *Tzedakah* is an additional foundational pillar of Judaism, a vehicle to actualize the desire for *tikkun*.

FROM INDIVIDUAL REPAIR TO COMMUNAL HEALING

Up until the last few centuries, as has been shown, personal choice and autonomy were not pressing issues within the Jewish world. While valuing the uniqueness of each individual, Judaism traditionally placed the emphasis on the sacred community committed to fulfilling the will of God as determined by rabbis. There could be no wholeness for the individual if those around her felt incomplete or if the community was fractured.

Abraham Joshua Heschel writes about the assumptions underlying this approach:

> A Jew does not believe alone; he believes with the Community of Israel; he shares an insight of three thousand years of sacred Jewish history. Religious living is not a private concern. Our own life is a movement in the symphony of ages. We are taught to pray as well as to live in the first person plural, to do the good "in the name of all Israel." All generations are present in every generation. The community of Israel lives in every Jew. Every Jew, and the individual Jew, can survive only through intimate attachment to and involvement in the community.[1]

Within the communal framework, individual success is never viewed as an end in itself. Wealth or status are not signs of election in Judaism. Rather, equal distribution of property is mandated by the Torah: Moses promises each family its own plot of land in *Eretz Yisrael*. Later, the potential for equality is insured through a method of reconciling property holdings every fifty years:

> You shall make *kadosh* the fiftieth year. Proclaim a year of release/redistribution throughout the land for all the inhabitants, a jubilee year it will be for you, and each of you will return to the [family land] inheritance, and each to your family. (Leviticus 25:10-11)

Commenting on this verse, Gunther Plaut notes:

> This legislation, then, expresses a constructive social purpose, rooted in the religious conviction that all wealth is

God's. As a modern interpreter has put it: "Just as the Communist demand is succinctly formulated, 'None shall have property,' so the biblical formulation is, 'Everyone shall have property.'" To achieve this end, wealth must be periodically redistributed.[2]

Fundamental to the Jewish worldview, then, is the belief that all people should share in the earth's bounty. A caring community also expects its members to support and nurture each other. This obligation ranges from the rabbinical dictum "All Israel is responsible, one for the other,"[3] which links a person's very life to those of fellow Jews, to the stipulation that a person's possessions are to be shared with others. So a *midrash* explains:

> Let your house be open; let the poor be members of your household. Let a man's house be open to the north and to the south, the east and the west, even as Job's house was, for Job made four doors to his house, that the poor might not be troubled to go round the house, but that each would find an open door when approaching.[4]

EMULATING GOD

The image of human beings as partners with God is a recurring theme of this study. As unique and creative beings, men and women must strive to increase human dignity and freedom in the world. But there are Jewish traditions that demand even more: that people behave as they would expect God to behave. In a Jewish commentary on the Torah's appeal to men and women to "walk in God's ways," the principle of *imitatio Dei* is enunciated:

These are the ways of the Lord, God, merciful and gracious [taken from Exodus 34:6] . . . As God is called merciful, so should you be merciful; as the Holy One, blessed be God, is called gracious, so too should you be gracious. As God is called righteous (Psalm 11:7), so you too should be righteous.[5]

This is not a sweet but inert statement about the need to develop pious qualities. *Imitatio Dei* is a veritable call to human action, an admission by God that there is no justice in the world without human intervention.

A chasidic tradition offers insight into this view with the following story. A *rebbe* is asked, "If everything in the world exists for a reason, why would God create an atheist?" The *rebbe* answers: "There are times you should act as if there is no God at all. If you see a man starving, do not think that God will provide. Feed the man! If a woman is in want of clothing and shelter, you must lift her up and furnish her with all she needs. You must not wait even a moment for God to act."

The act of caring for other human beings is called the *mitzvah* of *tzedakah*. Maimonides declares its centrality in Jewish life:

We are obligated to be more scrupulous in fulfilling the *mitzvah* of *tzedakah* than any other positive *mitzvah*. We are obligated because *tzedakah* is the sign of the righteous.[6]

Maimonides understands that *tzedakah* means more than ensuring the health and welfare of the poor and the needy. He recognizes that a community is judged best by how it deals with those who live on its fringes—by its commitment to expand the "image of God" to an ever-increasing number of people. *Tzedakah*, like *kedushah*, is at the core of a just Jewish society. It moves Jews on the path from a personal and familial *tikkun* to one which attends to the needs of the larger world.

JEWS FIRST?

The most fundamental Jewish principles of *tzedakah* derive from the belief that human beings are created in God's image. If greater dignity, freedom, and uniqueness are among the divine attributes each individual should possess, Jews have the responsibility to provide their fellow men and women with the basic necessities that will allow them to embody those attributes. The Torah explains *tzedakah* simply and directly:

> If, however, there is a needy person among you, one who resides in any of your settlements in the land that the Lord your Eternal is giving you, do not harden your heart and shut your hand against your needy fellow human being. Rather, you must open your hand and lend to that person sufficient for whatever is needed. (Deuteronomy 15:7-8)

Notice that these words do not speak about tithing or legislation, but go to the very heart of a caring community. All Israelites should be able to agree on what *tzedakah* is necessary and appropriate, the Torah seems to say, for they experienced the degradation of slavery in Egypt. The Torah, recorded in God's name, is Israel's shared consensus about what is just, fair, and worthwhile.

Maimonides, the most significant compiler of the traditions of *tzedakah*, analyzes the *mitzvah*'s requirements:

You are commanded to give the poor person whatever is needed. If he has no clothing, he should be provided with clothes; if she has no household furniture, it should be procured for her; if he has no wife, he should be helped to get married; if it is an unmarried woman, she should be provided with a husband. Though you are commanded to relieve a person's needs, you are not obligated to make the person rich.[7]

Tzedakah is a correction of something that is skewed. The world is dangerously imbalanced when there is poverty, starvation, homelessness, and sickness. Moses Cordovero, who with his pious customs in Tzefat sought to advance the redemption, declared: "A person would donate *tzedakah* every day so as to effect atonement for any sins, as it says, 'Rectify one's sins with *tzedakah*' (Daniel 4:24)."[8] Cordovero understood the essence of the Jewish idea of redemption: that there is no personal salvation if others are left behind. Human suffering must be ameliorated, preferably at the very moment it is witnessed.

True, one never knows if a single act is enough to bring the messiah, yet Judaism has traditionally viewed the process of redemption as a gradual and difficult process. Change is incremental; healing all the suffering in the world takes time. The classic code of medieval Jewish law, the *Shulhan Arukh*, presents a hierarchy of *tzedakah*, in which the righteous act expands in widening bands from the personal to the communal to the stranger:

The poor of one's [own] city take precedence over the poor of another city. The needy of Israel receive priority over the poor of the Diaspora. Obligations to local resident poor precede those owed to transient poor who have just come into the city. One's impoverished family members come before another poor person. Parents have priority over ... children [who can support themselves]. One's self comes before anyone else [all things being equal].[9]

Choices must be made in life, the passage reiterates. There may well be a shortage of grain seed or dialysis machines, a limit on the number of jobs or places in special schools. The author of the *Shulhan Arukh*, Yosef Karo, knows better than we do that there are limits to human capacity. With all of our advances in healing the sick, clothing the naked, and feeding the hungry, triage is still a necessary responsibility for those who allocate scarce resources.

The text just cited may seem terribly parochial, lacking the proper universalistic impulse, but Karo's steps contain a deep logic. Reuven Kimelman notes:

> The mutual helpfulness which takes place within the family sets the pattern for idealized relationships throughout society. Through ever-expanding circles of responsibility, we learn to reach out to the human family. Although charity begins at home, justice begins next door. Judaism is the training ground for creating consciousness of a mega-family which will ultimately incorporate all of humanity.[10]

Jews have put this approach into practice in various ways. The State of Israel's Law of Return gives any Jew or relative of a Jew automatic citizenship while forcing others to wait. In the years before the collapse of the Soviet Union, Jews around the world organized to liberate Soviet Jews. Israeli ingenuity and Jewish dollars rescued Ethiopian Jews from starvation and attack by flying them to the State of Israel. Jews have founded hospitals and community centers, private schools and clubs meant exclusively for Jews. Significant as such actions are, there are times when the Jewish community's preoccupation with Jews causes deep discomfort. Is this the fulfillment of Isaiah's dream?

> And the many peoples shall go and say:
>> Come, Let us go up to the Mount of the Lord,
>> To the House of the God of Jacob;
>> That God may instruct us all in God's ways,
>> That we may walk in God's path. (Isaiah 2:3)

Committed to changing the inequalities in all societies, the Jewish traditions that describe Israel as a nation of priests would claim that "modeling" behavior is the most effective means of improving the human condition. If Caucasian Jews of America whose families came from Europe spend hundreds of millions of dollars to safely settle black Ethiopian Jews in Israel, the theory goes, perhaps the Muslims, Christians, socialists, and animists of the world will protect their communities in Ethiopia as well. As a result, all Ethiopians will be cared for. The Joint Distribution Committee, a Jewish organization dedicated to protecting Jews around the world, arranged for an evacuation of Bosnian Jews from encircled Sarajevo. In the process, they also evacuated hundreds of Muslims and Christians. However, as winter intensified and thousands more lay vulnerable, European and Muslim nations merely continued to call for negotiations and further discussions. To be a "light unto the nations" means showing others how to care first for one's own family and community while remaining on the path of caring for the whole world. Perhaps there is a better or more effective approach, but as of the end of the twentieth century, none has been found.

TZEDEK AS A PATH TO UNIVERSAL WHOLENESS

The Jewish understanding of *tzedakah*, in fact, does not end with the sole care of Jews, any more than a person's concern for others should end with his or her own nuclear family. Since the goal is *tikkun olam*—the healing redemption of the world—all of humanity must be the object of care. So these words in the Torah's Holiness Codes come as no surprise:

> When a stranger resides with you in your land, you shall not wrong him. The stranger who resides with you shall be to you as one of your citizens; you shall love that person as yourself, for you were strangers in the land of Egypt; I am the Eternal your God. (Leviticus 19:33-34)

There is more to remembering slavery than sitting around a Passover *seder* table. The miracle of the Exodus liberation calls for a revolution—even if the changes unfold but one step at a time. The Rabbis, careful readers of the Torah, extended the obligation of concern to the non-Jew when they codified the traditions of *tzedakah*:

> The poor of the heathens are not prevented from gathering the left over and forgotten sheaves of grain as well as the corners of the field—all this in the interest of peace. Our Rabbis have taught: We support the poor of the heathen along with the poor of Israel, we visit the sick of the heathen along with the sick of Israel, and bury the poor of the heathen along with the poor of Israel, in the interests of peace.[11]

Maimonides adds that "one should find employment for heathens as one would with Jews, for the sake of peace."[12]

The same Torah that commands Jews to put idolaters to death here demands that they be included as equal participants of *tzedek* in the world, for only then can peace (translated also as "wholeness") be obtained. In an ironic twist, Rabbi Hiyya states in the Talmud: "One who turns the eyes away from *tzedakah* is as one who worships idols."[13]

Tzedakah, then, must be extended universally. The principles of *tzedakah* are meant to alter the conduct of nations as well as individuals in order to bring about a change in the human condition. The rabbinic language that connotes this is "for the sake of peace." Although separated by some three thousand years, the words of the Torah, the Rabbis, and Maimonides indicate that peace between all human beings is at the core of the Jewish vision, that there can be no peace if some human beings cannot sustain themselves, and that actively accepting the responsibility of *tzedakah* brings increasingly greater *kedushah* into the world.

RECONCILING THE TORAH'S JUSTICE
AND THE JUSTICE OF NATIONS

J. P. M. Walsh analyzes the words *tzedek* and the word *mishpat* as they are used in the biblical vision of community building. *Mishpat*, he explains, refers to the rule of law or of kings, the uses of power, the debates that take place in parliaments, tribal councils, and stockholders' meetings. Someone or somebody must exercise *mishpat* in a society, for without it, there is no means of governance.

> *Mishpat* is central to our existence as human beings, both individually and societally: we seek to have the say about

things, and others figure in that effort, especially as we participate in—or are excluded from—political structures.[14]

He continues by explaining that a community must build a consensus about how it will work, what is a sensible means of organizing society, and who will do what within the society. Traditions and a shared vision of the "real" world help to structure that consensus and mediate it to the next generation. At the heart of this communal accord is a sense that the way the community works is right, just, meaningful, and worthwhile. This sense Walsh defines as *tzedak(ah)*:

> *Tzedek* is usually translated "justice" and sometimes "righteousness," but as with *mishpat* those translations are limp. . . . No, *tzedek* means "rightness" (and can also mean *what* is right). . . . We go along, then, with what we are told to do because it seems right to us. We accept someone's exercise of *mishpat* because it seems to us to accord with *tzedek*. And that sense of *tzedek* is mediated to us by our participation in our community, as it also defines the consensus that holds a community together.[15]

A healthy society is one where the structures of authority that govern are in harmony with the values, ideals, and goals of the population being governed. In the language of Walsh's analysis, *mishpat* is consonant with *tzedek*. But what if political systems are corrupt and police states terrorize their citizens? What if communities validate behaviors and beliefs that diminish the qualities of human dignity and freedom? In this age of relativity, few are willing to judge another. As the United Nations repeatedly declares, there is no intrinsic right to interfere in the internal affairs of other nations. Jewish traditions that call on human beings to subvert the absolute truths of the compact majority flatly reject an "I'm okay, you're okay" philosophy. T*zedakah* demands more.

Judaism maintains that "just" and "unjust" are not relative concepts, that there is a moral compass implanted within humanity that knows how to separate the two. All the rationalizations of kings and presidents, priests, dictators, and academics throughout history do not shake our sense that to enslave, institutionalize, or murder innocent human beings cannot be what the Torah meant by *tzedakah*. Maimonides proclaims the covenantal challenge in spreading *tzedakah* when he states: "The throne of Israel is established and the religion of truth upheld only through *tzedakah*."[16]

Jews have a history of challenging the accepted *mishpat* of the nations in which they live, if only by expecting and demanding the right to be different. Walsh quotes the ancient victory song of the judge Deborah, verses proclaiming the collapse of the Canaanite oppressors:

> From the report of the recruiters,
>   between drawings of water,
>   there they chant the *tzedek(ot)* of God,
>   the *tzedek(ot)* of God's peasant warriors.
>   (Judges 5:11)

The news is proclaimed in all the villages of Canaan, among the serfs and oppressed peasants, that the *tzedek* of God and not the corrupt *mishpat* of the idolatrous Canaanite kings is victorious. The ragged band of Israelite warriors has overthrown the chariots of King Jabin's power. "Thrones are tottering. Pass the word. Join us," they proclaim.[17]

This tradition is carried on by the prophets of Israel who decry the *mishpat* even of the kings and priests of the Israelite nations. Jeremiah attacks the policies of injustice enforced by the governing elites of the Kingdom of Judah:

> Ha! he who builds his house without *tzedek*
> And his high chambers then without *mishpat*,
> Who makes his fellow human being work without pay
> And does not give him his wages. . . .
> Do you think you are more a king
> Because you compete in precious cedar?
> (Jeremiah 22:13-14)

A government that ignores the consensus of its people and of their traditions about what is just and fair will lose the allegiance of its citizens. To abandon the *tzedek* that links the people to God and both to the covenant is ultimately suicidal. There is no hope for those who think their own devisings can compete with the *tzedek* shared by God and the people of Israel. Jeremiah returns with a prophecy of destruction, echoing the words of Leviticus to the king:

> Assuredly, thus said the Eternal: You would not obey Me and proclaim a release/redistribution, each to his kinsman and countryman. Lo! I proclaim your release—declares the Eternal—to the sword, to disease, and to famine; and I will make you a horror to all the kingdoms of the earth. (Jeremiah 34:17)

One must not misinterpret the prophets. They are calling for harmony between the *tzedek* of God, which Jews have a moral obligation to embrace because of their unique experience, and the *mishpat* of those who legislate and rule. The prophets and later the Rabbis seek the improvement of government, however incrementally, not its eradication. It is through human efforts to improve the laws of the land and see to their just application that the world will be repaired. Mordecai Yitzhak Levi has this comment on the story in the Torah of how the tribal forces of Amalek attacked the Israelites in the desert, killing the vulnerable women and children:

> Had the children of Israel not forgotten about the slower ones in back but instead, brought them closer under the protecting wings of God's Presence, binding the slower to all of Israel, the Amalekites would not have succeeded in their attack. But because you allowed the slower ones to be "*aharekha*" (means both "behind you" and "other"), that you separated them off from you and made them "other," and you forgot about your brothers and sisters, Amalek could viciously attack them. Therefore, the Torah tells us to remember Amalek, so that we never forget to bring our brothers and sisters who need special attention into our midst.[18]

As a religious community dedicated to *tikkun olam*, it is not enough to protect one's family nor even one's community. Jews are encouraged by the rabbis to seek "the ways of peace" with all human beings, even idolaters, if that can help bring about the triumph of life over death, of goodness over evil. To accept the *mitzvah* of *tzedakah* is to take the activist's path and commit oneself to bringing on the revolution imagined by the Exodus, leading to the day when *tzedek* and *mishpat* will be one and the same.

10

Choosing Life in the Twenty-First Century

It is the middle of the night and a young child wakes up from a nightmare crying, "Mommy, Daddy!" Parents fly into the room, press the sobbing child to themselves, feel the shuddering fear, and soothingly say, "Don't worry. Everything is going to be all right." The child is calmed and gently falls back asleep. Peter Berger, the sociologist of religion, then asks the question: "Were the parents lying?"

Living with Uncertainty: Is Anything Not Relative?

Such questions constantly hover over us, coloring the ways that we see the world and the ways in which we live our lives. Our rational, disciplined self says that the parents *are* lying, since they cannot predict the future nor can they truly protect their child. Today, we know more about nightmarish evil than any generation in human history, more than we wish to comprehend. I imagine one of my own children trying to

129

reach me from a Nazi children's transport during the Holocaust. Could I have said, "Don't worry, everything will be all right?" Then I remember the time I sat with a vibrant Jewish woman dying of cancer. It was Friday afternoon and, with guitar, wine, and bread, I introduced her to *Shabbat*—the first *Shabbat* she had celebrated in her life. When I was about to leave, she said, "This was wonderful. I'll remember it forever." I felt as if I had been slapped. In a few days she would die; what is the satisfaction and meaning of *forever*?

Whether or not the parents were lying and what *forever* means cannot be answered by scientific investigations. The things in life that people cherish most, that move them to tears or ecstasy, are not objectively valuable or positive. Each person learns and, ultimately, chooses to make them that way. That is not to say that there is no predisposition in human beings toward moral behavior or behavior that is intrinsically meaningful. Perhaps over the generations of human evolution, those who struggled to increase and improve life produced more offspring who survived and flourished, thus favoring an affirmation of life. And, in fact, a backlash, both visceral and intellectual, has been forming against the modern presumption that moral character and supportive community-building are no more than learned attributes resulting from effective socialization. James Q. Wilson argues that morality is an inherent characteristic of the human species. He notes that research is discovering that there are universal standards of fairness, sympathy, self-control, and duty:

> They emerge from serious reflection about why we insist upon judging, morally, events and people around us. Students of child development have observed the emergence of the moral sense and given respectful and thoughtful ac-

counts of it . . . scientific findings provide substantial support for its existence and power.[1]

Certainly, the Jewish texts on creation assert that there are behaviors and values that are inherently "good," that a sense of "rightness" or justice can be universally shared. Judaism claims that human beings do know what *tzedek* means and when it has been achieved. Tears and laughter, empathy with another's pain or joy, can transcend cultural divides. At the same time, personal, familial, and communal expressions of morality and justice vary from individual to individual and from community to community. In Jewish language, God's image should and does refract into multiple and rich diversity.

How do the values of a particular community direct behavior and maintain their influence in an age of such openness and choices? In the past, it was presumed that the specific and unique responses to life nurtured by a culture were passed on through the process of socialization, whereby a child was decisively inducted into the traditions of his or her family and community. But it is clear that in contemporary North America, no culture retains the monolithic control it formerly had in shaping a child's values and allegiances. The myriad lifestyle options available invest each individual with a radical sense of autonomy. Each person must *choose* a path to make life rich and meaningful. Yet, confronting the infinite possibilities, confidence in any one of them may waver. Faced with the freedom to choose, we paradoxically may become too paralyzed to live our own lives. That is why, in an age of unparalleled scientific and social improvements, so many feel that the quality of their lives is eroding.

Communities and their cultures are expected to answer

questions about the nature of human existence. The answer offered may be no more complicated than "It is God's will," or "It always was this way." But when the events of a person's life cannot be explained by the language and faith statements of the community, doubts and desertion result. A society with all its hoary traditions that cannot provide meaning and purpose for its adherents will eventually fail to sustain itself.

Indeed, the loss of faith in traditional religious answers to the most personal existential questions has been the hallmark of the modern age. Marshall Berman points out that the revolutionary overthrow of traditions is a symptom of modernity, not its cause. The fundamental changes in social relations, means of production, technological advances, methods of communication, and communal organization produce perpetual uncertainty, he explains. The rate of change is so rapid that change itself becomes the only reliable tradition. Berman then cites a vision projected more than a century ago by Karl Marx, the ultimate rootless man:

> All fixed, fast-frozen relations, with their train of ancient and venerable prejudices and opinions, are swept away, all new-formed ones become antiquated before they can ossify. All that is solid melts into air, all that is holy is profaned, and men at last are forced to face . . . the real conditions of their lives and their relationships with their fellow men.[2]

Whole elaborately constructed civilizations have fallen before our eyes; the most articulate propaganda could not protect their spiritual bankruptcy. And if religious communities cannot provide compelling answers to the transformations of modernity and the challenges this imposes on meaningfulness, they will atrophy and die.

The Jewish Experience in America

Imagine a contemporary *bat mitzvah* or wedding party, or perhaps a special birthday party or anniversary. The family is dressed in the trendiest styles, an eclectic mix of African, European, and Indian influences. Many of the guests have flown in from around the world; those who couldn't do so sent in their congratulations by phone, electronic mail, or fax. The decor is international, each table set with a different cultural theme. The cuisine is international as well, as is the entertainment; the band mixes reggae with Broadway musicals, rock music with ethnic dance medleys. The party includes the recitation of a Native American poem, followed by a religious prayer and a favorite folk song. When the honoree rises to acknowledge the moment, one can only wonder if she has any idea who she or anyone else in the room truly is.

The contemporary world of autonomy and choice confuses us with a hunger to taste and smell and touch everything within our grasp. But therein lies a deep fallacy, for human beings may dream in universals, but real life is lived in particulars. A person cannot live as a universal human being. One is not a friend of every person; one's life is filled with specific relationships with distinct individuals. One may dream of falling in love in a generic way, but passion is felt in relation to a concrete, complex other person. The things that count most in life are experienced in direct, personal relationships, whether they be with a mother and father, friends and spouse, one's people, or one's God.

We may wish that we could touch and taste every tradition from every community, as well as fantasize about being born in another time or place. But the reality is that each of us has already been molded by the family and community in which we were raised, and that has invariably affected how we think and dream. That upbringing need not necessarily define a person for life, but one must recognize that to know the self, to feel authentic, one must know from whence he or she has come.

Children who are offered a mélange of cultural traditions actually are being given none at all: they are being told to pick out their favorite bits and construct their own. This is an incredible deprivation. With no clear personal or communal identity, they develop no commitment to the past, no binding ties to any particular worldview, no grounding in any culture's understanding of what it means to live an ethical life. Kenneth Gergen pinpoints the damage done:

> As we begin to incorporate the dispositions of the varied others to whom we are exposed, we become capable of taking their positions, adopting their attitudes, talking their language, playing their roles. In effect, one's self becomes populated by others. The result is a steadily accumulating sense of doubt in the objectivity of any position one holds. . . . In the face of continuous point and counterpoint—both in public and private spheres—one slowly approaches the awareness that perhaps the monument of objectivity is hollow.[3]

Although the modernity of the last century lost its credibility by failing to deliver on its lofty promises, the universalistic impulse that propelled it remains alive today. For the most part, however, it remains unfulfilled. The cultural products of North American life, from television and other passive forms of entertainment to public education and popular music, provide ambiguous and problematic support for personal and communal meaning. With no particular person, community, or culture to love and cherish, people increasingly seem to love and cherish nothing in particular.

In their initial encounter with North American life, Jews relentlessly tried to adapt themselves and their Judaism to the pluralist, open, and democratic character of the United States and Canada. Most basic was the urge to "make it," to provide for the elemental needs of the family. Even before they could speak English, the immigrants at the turn of the century transferred their drive to escape spiritual and physical suffering in Europe into achieving the American success story. Before the world could be redeemed, families had to be fed and children prepared for making it in America.

Yet, with all their material deprivation, Jewish communities at the turn of the century, and the families which composed them, were purposeful institutions. The synagogue, study hall, social-support agencies, and the Jewish home itself molded character and relationships. Children were expected to accept responsibility for their extended family as well as for society at large. They were taught a civil form of *mitzvot*: seeking to elevate their lives and the condition of the world with acts of what their parents had known as *kedushah*. In the past century, Jewish children grew up to be lawyers, doctors, teachers, and philanthropists, because they were imbued with an awareness that there was healing to be done and they were endowed with the capacity and commitment to act on that awareness. The good they did determined their success.

Yet the immigrant Jewish family that pushed its members to the limit also had its downside. The overpowering Jewish mother and the boorish but financially successful father became figures of parody. Joseph Telushkin, in a chapter from his book *Jewish Humor*, "Oedipus, Shmedipus, As Long As

He Loves Me," relates the story of the Jewish mother who bragged of her son's devotion: "Can you imagine," she gushes to her friends, "what a son I have! He spends a hundred dollars a week at his therapist just talking about me."[4] In a scathing attack on the Jewish-American family, Philip Roth in *Portnoy's Complaint* tells how a "good boy" driven by guilt leaves for a European vacation with his Christian lover to escape the suffocation he feels at home:

> "But in Europe where—?" he calls after me, as the taxi pulls away from the curb. "I don't know where," I call after him, gleefully waving farewell. I am thirty three, and free at last of my mother and father. For a month.
> "But how will we know your address?"
> Joy! Sheer joy! "You won't!"
> "But what if in the meantime—?"
> "What if what?" I laugh. "What if what are you worried about now?"
> "What if—?" And my God, does he really actually shout it out the taxi window? Is his fear, his greed, his need and belief in me so great that he actually shouts these words out into the streets of New York? "What if I die?"[5]

The invasive parents of caricature and analysts' couches may well be a distortion of the first-generation Jewish family in America. Yet one of the most important functions of the Jewish family was to transmit the covenantal commitment to transform the world. To do so, it was necessary to become a success, for Judaism is committed to this-world improvements that require energy, money, and the power to get things done. The immigrant parents living during the Depression years never became "real" Americans; most could barely survive the rigors of daily life. The pressure on the next generation to succeed, to make it in America and be a credit to the parents' struggles and to the Jewish people, must have been overwhelming. Children became *nachas* machines, a salve for the incompleteness of the Jewish-American dream. And, as much as the children of the immigrants protested, they too were consumed with achievement: to prove to mama and papa that the struggle was worthwhile and to enable their parents to enjoy, at least vicariously, their successes.

And succeed they did. In one generation, Jews moved solidly into the professional middle class and became the most educated ethnic group in North America. By force of persistent pressure and will and talent, they broke down barriers, entered all professions, and moved to every part of the country. In race-conscious America, they increasingly seemed like the comfortable majority. What could be more evocative of Jewish status in America than, when asked on the last United States Federal Census form to indicate "identity" out of the huge number of possible categories available (Black, Hispanic, Native American, Samoan, Aleut), Jews could only mark "Caucasian"? Today's Jews are demographically most like Scandinavians, part of the North American elite.

This is more than the result of financial stability. When the actor Walter Matthau, who is only part Jewish, was asked why he identifies as a Jew when it would be so easy to be a Christian, he replied, "I am a social climber." Jews have status in North America. For an all-American Christian girl or boy to marry a Jew is not a tragedy, it is often an opportunity: Jewish men are perceived to be good providers and fathers who respect their wives. Jewish women are seen as bright and talented, excelling in all they do even as they create wonderful homes.

But the costs of this generation's accomplishments were enormous. It is now clear that the adaptations required to "make it"—spiritually, ethically, socially, and financially—were unbearable for many Jews. They fled the traditional home, with its covenantal demands and overwhelming responsibilities.

I heard some of their frustration and hurt during a lecture I delivered in a small southwestern town. As I rhapsodized about the Jewish role of healing the world, one very successful son of immigrants demanded that I shut up with the words: "I have enough pressures in my life to be told that the fate of the Jewish people and the world rests on my shoulders." Other first-generation Americans, many of whom were now living in suburban communities, deliberately avoided re-creating in their own homes the world of their fathers and mothers.

The *mitzvot* that molded the character of the Jews were either streamlined or abandoned. Torah study was discarded, replaced with secular learning and university education. By their language, dress, pleasures, and celebrations, Jews became practically indistinguishable from other Americans in their socioeconomic class. Now that their position in American society was assured, Jews increasingly were challenged to explain why they should identify as Jews rather than follow the model (at least of the higher social classes) of integration into the majority all-American Caucasian population.

In abandoning their distinct behaviors and traditional responsibilities, more may have been lost than vague memories of chicken soup with *matzah* balls and family dinners on Passover. The generation of Jews that strove so hard to be American also lost the traditions of a community whose members cared intensely about each other, shared values, and collectively pushed to improve the world. It was easy to forget the connection between freedom and the wandering in the desert, where Jews had learned to be subversives. The new generation of Jews lost interest in their role as liberators.

This is not meant to be an attack on the United States or Canada. North Americans are good, decent, and caring people, and Jews should and will participate in these societies. But to identify so completely with America to the point of abandoning their own covenantal vision is a form of idolatry. For there still is much to be done. Divorce rates and abuse continue to rise in Jewish as well as non-Jewish families. Projections are that well over half of all American children will spend at least part of their lives in a single-parent home. Drug rehabilitation and Alcoholics Anonymous programs are overflowing and elderly parents are abandoned by their families. These are the staples of social-service agency caseloads and clerical counseling, and indeed of society at large.

The inner pains felt by so many children, teenagers, and adults, in spite of their affluence and success, must give American Jews pause in their flight from Jewish traditions. Typically, communities cherish those traditions that nurture shared values and behaviors and shed those that are dissonant. In America, however, Jewish behaviors and values as expressed in *mitzvot* were discarded wholesale, yet the product was not what most anticipated. The irony is that while American Jews have won full public acceptance, in their own homes and in their own souls, many feel like strangers. It is precisely in the nuclear family or in the life lived alone that upwardly mobile Jews feel they have been most severely threatened. Harold Schulweis writes:

Jewish idealism and altruism and respect for the complexity of life and the need to find meaning beyond narcissism are threatened from within. . . . The internal threats of the vacuous Jewish family [are] more prosaic than the challenges from alien ideologies but they are more dangerous precisely because they are the constant gnawing away at the Jewish moral and spiritual fiber within the family.[6]

The recent malaise of personal, familial, and communal life has brought a call to reevaluate the traditions of *kedushah*, *mitzvot*, *tzedakah*, and *tikkun olam*.

REIMAGINING THE FUTURE

Throughout this book, we have explored how Jews nurtured a belief that life is valuable, that the world is good, and that humans have a need and responsibility to increase sacredness. It is now time to address the most fundamental question: whether the Jewish story can be reimagined for this age in light of the assaults discussed in this chapter.

The problem for most individuals living in North America at the turn of the millennium is that so many of the stories of the past, and the resulting political and social systems, each with its own traditions and legal structures, seem to be discredited. The narrative of meaning handed down from generations past no longer compels. Its traditions do not seem relevant to a modern world spinning with options. "Modern man is afflicted with a permanent identity crisis, a condition conducive to considerable nervousness," says Peter Berger.[7] Even as we may envy the comforting clarity of our great-grandparents' world, we recognize that there is no return.

And North American culture is with us too, in all of its dizzying choices and rich pluralism. It is not a retreat that is called for but a new engagement. There can be no refuge from the anxieties of abundance, autonomy, and freedom itself, for the doubts and anxieties go hand in hand with a secular world of multiple visions. Choices, even silent ones, will be made. To say that the world makes sense, that there is order in the universe, or that life is better than death cannot be proven. To wake up in the morning and know that the sun will shine and that the day will be filled with excitement, perhaps with joy, rather than with darkness and fear, is to make an existential, deeply personal choice. Above all, you are now challenged in your soul: Can you celebrate the journey that is life with exhilaration, filled with purpose, flexibility, and strength, or will you experience panic and paralysis? This is the test. As the chasidic masters said so well: "The world is a very narrow bridge; the essence of life is not to be overwhelmed by fear."

The end of the twentieth century has jarred the post-Holocaust Jew with a double assault: the abject loss of traditional faith in God and Torah as well as a faltering faith in the liberal ethic of liberty, equality, and fraternity. Chastened by the magnitude of the destruction—not only of life, but of confidence in their Jewish heritage and in the truths of Western civilization—Jews have been left feeling orphaned. If the covenant is to continue, as Irving Greenberg noted, it must be voluntarily and self-consciously chosen by Jews who know the evidence of their history yet still embrace a commitment to *kedushah* through *mitzvot*. Jews must be so in love with their dream of *tikkun olam* that they will choose a life of *kedushah* and *mitzvot*, not in an isolated ghetto, but in the midst of the richness of North American culture. And the impact of this revitalized and vibrant Jewish community will help nurture and redirect the same

American culture that presently poses such a powerful threat to Jewish self-identity.

Modern Jews are not bereft of models of commitment that will play well in the contemporary age. Within Judaism are deep and abiding traditions that unite personal choice to a covenantal partnership of responsibility. Irwin Kula states:

> The narrative context enables us to explore imaginatively what it might mean for us to perform this or that action. Unless we can enlarge our own perspective through an imaginative encounter with the experience of others; unless we can participate empathetically in the experiences of Abraham and Sarah and Miriam and Moses and Rabbi Yohanan Ben Zakkai and Maimonides and Herzl and Sammy and David . . . their suffering, pain, frustrations as well as their joy, fulfillment, plans, hopes and dilemmas; unless we can let our values and ideas be called into question from various points of view, we cannot develop a *halakhah* (a Jewish pathway).[8]

There is the memory of Abraham challenging God to do justice and Sarah fighting to save her child as the transmitter of the Covenant. There is a voice at Mount Sinai declaring the love relationship between God and Israel. Slaves of Egypt and desert wandering become priests and monarchs struggling to create a different type of nation in *Eretz Yisrael*. Poets sing odes of victory and prophets doom Israel to suffering and destruction. There are laws and psalms, stories and prayers, disputation and legends. From these words and images emerge the subtleties and nuances of Jewish identity, the self-definition this people takes on its long journey. From this past, Jews locate the powerful traditions that challenge and compel them to hear God's voice and experience their lives as commanded. As Robert Cole notes so well:

This story, yours, mine—it's what we all carry with us on this trip we take, and we owe it to each other to respect our stories and learn from them.[9]

The Torah relates that God says to the Israelites: "I give you today life and death, the blessing and the curse. Therefore, choose life" (Deuteronomy 30:19). It is not physical existence that now hangs in jeopardy, but the type of lives human beings will create for themselves.

As was evident from the chapters on Jewish history, the understandings of *tikkun* and of *mitzvah* evolved in complex responses to the events and ideas of their time. In this age, it is no less complex to choose the *mitzvot* that make each person a partner in repairing the world. There are, of course, broad outlines of what being Jewish means, blueprints from prior ages. But there are so many issues to consider freshly that it is difficult to have full confidence that any choice is the right one. That is both the anguish and the thrill of living in an age of transformation. Three examples will suffice to describe some of the challenges:

Social Justice and Social Change

In the formative period of biblical Judaism, God was the agent of change in the world and the source of all that was to be blessed. But already in the rabbinic age, the sages could imagine a different relationship, where human beings were the partners of God in initiating change. Limited in real power, though not in their vision of human potential, the Rabbis taught:

"Follow the Lord your God" (Deuteronomy 13:5)—what does that mean? Is it possible for a mortal to follow God's

Presence? The verse comes to teach us that we should follow the attributes of the Holy One Praised Be God. As God
clothes the naked, so you should clothe the naked. The Bible
teaches that the Holy One visited the sick; You should visit
the sick. The Holy One comforted those who mourn; You
should comfort those who mourn. The Holy One buried the
dead; You should bury the dead.[10]

The Jewish tradition of *tzedakah* demands that Jews care
for those among them who are weaker. But herein lies the
challenge of modernity. Because the human capacity to pre-
vent starvation, provide basic medical care, move whole
populations, and educate masses of former illiterates is so
much greater today, so too is human responsibility to do
more. And Jews are now in the political and economic posi-
tions to affect policies of social change as never before in
history.

Some of the old, once obvious solutions no longer work.
Acting like God to improve the quality and quantity of life
has proven remarkably difficult—much like what God faced
when creating a world of autonomous human beings. In the
beginning of the century, Jews embraced liberalism almost
automatically because conservatives supported king, church,
and the military—the institutions that still sought to suppress
Jews and Judaism—and because liberals opposed fascism.
Even after Jews achieved solid middle-class status, they continued to support political institutions and candidates who
promoted civil rights and social concern. As Milton Himmel-
farb noted decades ago, Jews "live like Episcopalians and vote
like Hispanics."

Yet voting like Hispanics has not solved the ills of North
America. As one surveys the social and economic landscape

of life in the United States, there is reason for deep concern. In spite of (or, some claim, because of) progressive social policies, the real conditions of many blacks, minorities, poor people, and children have deteriorated. It often seems that the very policies of social justice that reflect the highest values of *tzedakah* undermined *tzedek* itself. Promoting individual rights and limiting the right of the government or others to forcibly institutionalize those who are mentally ill, for example, may be one reason that homelessness has increased. In spite of educational programs that teach responsible sex in public schools and the distribution of free birth control, the number of teenage pregnancies has increased for the population at large. Assuring the right of an adolescent girl to have an abortion without parental knowledge or consent protects her civil rights but may well undermine the family, just as a government that supports unemployed single mothers with cash payments may be creating a permanent underclass.

This is not an attempt to discredit the liberal impulse of North American Jewry or to pretend that other policies would have better solved the social ills that undermine *tzedek* in the United States and Canada. Rather, it is to point out that the Jewish capacity to challenge accepted norms disappears when Jews become so linked to one movement or party that uniquely *Jewish* insights into social organization are ignored or dismissed. My grandfather knew how to pull the lever marked "Democratic Party" and never veered from voting a straight party ticket until he died. I was brought up to see Judaism as synonymous with liberal values and politics. Although I am grateful for this social-activist tradition, I nevertheless feel obligated to reevaluate political and social policy absolutes that may have become "idolatrous."

A debate among Jews over social policies in North America could provide new insights and promote more successful policy decisions. This already takes place when Jewish social-service institutions, founded at the turn of the century to help Americanize new Jewish immigrants while providing for their needs, no longer have a Jewish constituency. They must address whether Jewish agencies should develop and finance programs for the needy in their towns even if few are Jews, or should these institutions focus money and energy on other issues. If the government provides minimal resources for traditional social service concerns, does the money Jews pay in taxes fulfill their obligation to care for the needy among them? As Yosef Karo and Maimonides before him teach, responsible Jews must make serious choices. And democracy, power, and affluence now empower Americans to act and determine the future more than ever before in human history.

Leonard Fein artfully presents the challenge:

> The Jew as critic, the Jew as idealist. And now, invited to power, the Jew as a builder of the bridging connection between criticism and creation. The opportunity now, at long and painful last, is to go beyond dissent, beyond smashing the idols; it is also to mend the world so that it works as we've been taught it was meant to. . . . Criticism all by itself is acceptable only from the powerless. . . . So, also, idealism. One or the other, without painstaking attention to the gritty detail of construction, leads not to plowshares but to the guillotine.[11]

Yet we also are more modest. We are ending a century of grand ideological experiments. Perhaps the Jewish contribution to this discussion will be that the key to real transformation is a long-haul serious engagement in incremental *tikkun olam*. Not solutions, but small, helpful steps will be necessary. Not singular heroic acts, but collective, supportive experiments that address the painful social hemorrhaging that often seems to describe the present state of North American society—a form of social action *kedushah*, elevating behaviors and programs from mundane activity to sacred healing.

Debates in North America and within the Jewish community should be informed by the traditions of Judaism and the historical experience of the Jewish people, enriching the body of data from which decisions will be made. Painful as it may be for Jews to refine or even abandon medieval codes or more recent secular faiths, anything less is a serious and tragic diminution of the Jewish commitment to repair the world.

Human Life versus Human Dignity

My grandmother lies in the hospital, connected to life through tubes, monitors, and heart-sustaining equipment. She is loved and respected by her family, who feel protected by her presence. Energetic and caring medical practitioners can do little to help, save by supplying medication to reduce her discomfort. The hospital's social worker is present, but cannot relieve the anguish of her relatives. The hospital staff awaits our judgment to determine what further steps to take. Ethicists and theologians, just like you and me, have no objective criteria for when life has ended or what actions a family should take at these moments.

One Jewish tradition says that, since God created life and as humans are the most valued and loved of God's creations, then human life must be singularly valued. The more life can be extended, the better. This explains the legal decision that

> A person on the deathbed is like the living in every regard. . . . Whoever touches or moves the person, that one commits murder. Rabbi Meir would compare the dying person to a candle which is flickering; should a person touch it, it immediately goes out.[12]

Since the life-sustaining equipment available in hospitals today is meant to function indefinitely, the act of pulling a plug or removing a mask not only touches the person, but directly causes life to cease.

At the same time, Judaism deeply values human dignity, for each human being is created in God's image. Rabbis over the years constructed a formula that commands one to allow death to come mercifully:

> One may not prevent a person from dying quickly. If there are factors which prevent a speedy death, such as the noise of a person chopping wood outside the room in which the dying person lies, we remove the chopper from that location.[13]

A modern voice of tradition adds:

> Jewish law sanctions, and perhaps even demands, the withdrawl of any factor—whether extraneous to the patient or not—which may artificially delay his demise in the final phase.[14]

Jewish traditions once again speak in conflicting voices reflecting searing complexities the rabbis debated the past two thousand years. How do I then balance the passion for extending life with the knowledge that my grandmother would feel degraded and inhuman?

In prior ages, death came naturally. Increasingly, the moment of death is a decision made by patients, doctors, families, and society. If one seeks to do the act that is more *kadosh*—and, by so doing, strive to fulfill the obligation to improve the world—how can one determine whether or not to disconnect the life-support system?

THE QUESTION OF HOMOSEXUALITY

Few Jews today support laws that restrict the rights of homosexuals to enter any profession, participate in all aspects of society, and be accorded full civil rights. But how should homosexual behavior be viewed within the context of *mitzvot* that will lead to sacredness? If Judaism is taken seriously as a resource for addressing contemporary issues, Jewish responses to homosexuality must result from an internal debate that reacts with integrity to its essential traditions. It is within this framework that the question is posed whether homosexuals have a place within the orbit of Jewish life.

The Torah seems unequivocal in the verses pertaining to male lovemaking. God states:

Do not lie with a male as one lies with a woman; it is an abhorrence. (Leviticus 18:22)

If a man lies with a male as one lies with a woman, the two of them have done an abhorrent thing; they shall be put to death—the guilt of their own blood is upon them. . . . You shall not follow the practices of the nation that I am driving out before you. For it is because they did all these things that I abhorred them. . . . (Leviticus 20:13, 23)

Nowhere in any Jewish traditions, at least up until the last few decades of the twentieth century, can we find commentaries, texts, or codes that sanction male homosexuality, although there is a debate over lesbianism (for which there is no directly articulated Torah prohibition). It would be disingenuous to imply that Judaism ever validated overt homosexual behavior in the past.

But aside from forbidding homosexual relations, there is little discussion of the matter in Jewish texts. In one reference, the sages disagreed with a colleague's recommendation that two men not be allowed to sleep in the same bed because, they confidently asserted, there is no homosexuality among Jews. Because of the dearth of material on this matter, however, one can only conjecture as to why the traditions are so unequivocal.

One answer may be that homosexuality was not viewed as a loving relationship with someone of the same sex but, rather, as part of the pagan rituals or general sexual depravity of idolatrous cultures. What the Torah was forbidding, in other words, was the imitation of the corrupt nations that resided in *Eretz Yisrael* with the Israelites: "You shall not follow their practices." Since homosexual prostitution was once part of a degenerate society, the behavior itself was considered a Canaanite abomination. With that in mind, we have choices of how to look at homosexuality. We can see it as a contemporary example that parallels the biblical one of how core Jewish values are rejected for the vacuous American standard of "everything goes," and thus, the injunction must stand. Or, with new insights concerning the complexities of human sexuality, we can recognize that the homosexual couple is not a product of American decadence but two human beings expressing love no differently than heterosexuals.

Another approach is to look at the condemnation of homosexuality in light of the Torah's general understanding of sexuality. The essence of sexuality in the Torah is the male-female relationship, which emphasizes the distinctiveness of the two genders. In fact, biblical Judaism is consumed by distinctions: In creation, God divides light from dark, the waters below from the waters above. The animals are all categorized. Later in the Torah, Jews are forbidden to mix linen and wool in their clothing, to crossbreed or eat certain animals. Human dignity rests on the uniqueness of individuals, including respect for gender differentiation. For a man to lie with another man "as with a woman" is to rupture the distinct categories of gender. Would it make a difference if it became clear, based on physiological and psychological study, that there are men who will never be able to lie with a woman and whose identity as homosexuals is a true expression of their human uniqueness?

A third aspect of this dilemma is the value the Torah places on life and its view of procreation as fundamental to sexual expression. While lovemaking is encouraged even when a woman is pregnant or can no longer bear children (which means that sexual intercourse is certainly not solely for the purpose of conception), the act of sexual intercourse between a male and female is still symbolically linked to the potential for new life. When two men or two women make love, there is never a potential for new life. To knowingly build a sexual relationship that precludes creation undermines one of the core elements of sexual union. On the other hand, Jewish tradition accepts that a heterosexual couple which cannot have children or an individual who chooses to remain single can still be partners in the Jewish mission.

There is more, of course, to human relations than sexual compatibility and satisfaction. There may be shared intellectual, aesthetic, and emotional interests. Partners may care for and support each other in sickness or in sorrow. Such loving behavior heightens human dignity and elevates the image of God in the world. Today, when homosexual relationships are far more public than ever before, examples of such loving abound.

Two texts address such relationships between men (they can be easily adapted to two women as well). The first speaks of Jonathan, son of King Saul, and David, who eventually will become king. Both men are married and have children. Their love is so great that when Jonathan dies, David publicly declares: "I grieve for you, my brother Jonathan, you were most dear to me. Your love was wonderful to me, more than the love of women" (2 Samuel 1:26). Out of their relationship, the *Mishnah* determines a general principle:

> Any loving relationship which depends upon something, [when] that thing is gone, the love is gone. But any which does not depend upon something will never come to an end. . . . What is a loving relationship which does not depend upon something? That is the love for David and Jonathan.[15]

The second text is even more evocative of a close bond between two men. The writer comments on the expression, "Get yourself a *haver*, a friend":

> This teaches us that a person should set himself a companion, to eat with him, drink with him, study Bible with him, study Mishnah with him, sleep [in the same bed?] with him, and reveal to him all his secrets, secrets of Torah and secrets of worldly things.[16]

Here are traditions that view a relationship between two men (or two women) as very positive indeed. Both texts assume there is deep intimacy—from passionate study to shared secrets told late at night. The commitment of each to the other and a clear mutual respect is apparent. And human dignity is magnified by the love between them. Although love brings the two close together, the uniqueness of each is not jeopardized. Such a relationship between two individuals of the same sex, filled with shared support and loving, is easy to validate for according to Genesis, God recognizes that to be fully human means that "it is not good for a person to be alone" (Genesis 2:18).

A homosexual couple could well live out the ideals of Jonathan and David or of true *haverim*, friends. (One would be no less impressed with a heterosexual couple who could tender such loving.) Judaism could see these aspects of a relationship between two men or two women as an expansion of *kedushah* into new terrain. Steve Ashkenazy, who is involved in a synagogue that welcomes gay and lesbian members, writes:

As for the halachic prohibition against homosexuality, I think that there just couldn't be a law in Judaism that is impossible to follow. This is a very important guideline. It is impossible for me not to be what I am. . . . Judaism is against celibacy, which was seen as a deviation. It could keep you from studying Torah because of impure thoughts, fantasies, whatever, if you aren't fulfilled sexually. And a gay person cannot be fulfilled heterosexually. . . .

So even though the rabbis have interpreted the law in the way they have through the centuries, it can't really be a command of God. . . . That the Torah prohibits homosexual acts and that God has created me gay are two incontrovertible facts to me. Not allowing this one conflict to throw me off track is the challenge of my life.[17]

In these words you hear a modern voice continuing the struggle to locate himself within the orbit of *kedusha*, reconciling diverse traditions into a living Judaism.

One legacy of the Jewish past, emanating from the Torah's prohibitions, has been to see homosexuality as a threat to and a negation of the fundamental values of family, human dignity, and sacredness. But another legacy of our past is the assurance that God values the uniqueness of each human being and that the universe is fostering ever richer and more diverse forms of life. Within the love between two human beings, rather than in a bitter aloneness, is exactly where so many Jewish traditions say God resides. Yoel Kahn, the rabbi of a synagogue that reaches out to gay and lesbian Jews, writes:

The I–Thou relationship demands that we see each other not as an object but as a holistic person in the divine image. Because we are so vulnerable in these private relationships, we are uniquely challenged to practice ethical living and covenant respect in our lives. . . . The realization of our most intimate yearnings is not a closed circle that leads back to our partner; rather, the Jewish dialectic of personal and communal obligation turns us outward from the most intimate sphere to return and reengage in the labor of restoring and healing the world.[18]

I cannot predict the traditions that will emerge as Jews and Jewish communities struggle to define the nature of *kedushah* in same sex relationships. But the debate itself is an affirmation of Jewish vitality in this age of transformation.

CELEBRATING HUMAN INDETERMINACY

As much as people may seek simple and quick answers, they are not forthcoming. Modernity pushes us to the outer limits of moral judgment. People who take modernity seriously must struggle with the many questions that arise from extraordinary technological advances and new ways of understanding the world. Jews also must take into account the alternative values of North American society and allow them to influence Jewish decision-making. The attempt by some to coast along using premodern models, marshaling medieval codes and arguments to solve all contemporary questions, is understandable. Many of us, exhausted by the pressures of an ever-changing world, simply want to abide by conventional thinking or say we are willing to follow whatever someone else decides.

Seeking clarity through absolutes does not address the richness of our times, as the freedoms and pluralism predicted by the prophets and for which generations prayed unfold more fully than anyone dared to imagine. Mark Johnson elaborates:

> It takes no great insights to recognize that our moral understanding is complex, multidimensional, messy, anything but transparent and utterly resistant to absolutes and reductive strategies. This is not to say that we shouldn't seek as much clarity, determinateness, and stability as we can realistically manage . . . [but] we negotiate our way through this tangled maze of moral deliberation, one step at a time, never sure where we will end, guided only by our ideals of what we, and others, and our shared world might become.[19]

To live maturely in the modern world of radical and rapid change, people will have to accept indeterminacy and multiple alternatives—the anxiety of never making a decision with absolute certainty. Only the obligation is clear: If the world is to be healed, each person must be an active player in that process. And each person must take up the challenge of how to be part of the modern world yet separate enough to retain a critical role as subversive.

Within the context of a people that shares language, history, vision, and a sense of commitment, traditions live and speak within those who choose to be a part. The external behavioral demands and legal structures can never replace the experiential narrative that supports the story of one's own life and gives that life meaning. Alasdair MacIntyre explains:

Man is in his actions and practice . . . a story telling animal. He is not essentially, but becomes through his history, a teller of stories that aspire to truth. But the key question for men is not about their own authorship; I can only answer the question "What am I to do?" if I can answer the prior question "Of what story or stories do I find myself a part?"[20]

Jewish traditions speak in many voices to those dedicated to *kedushah*, providing narratives that test those committed to elevate their behavior to greater sacredness and their actions to a sense of *mitzvah*. The key to the present is that one not only inherits the stories of the past, but that each person has a story to add to the narrative of which he or she is a part.

With all the vicissitudes of history and the changing fortunes of Jews, the Jewish mission has stayed remarkably intact. It remains: to increase the liberation of the desert by subverting the self-serving stands of dictators, intellectual or religious orthodoxies, and even smug democratic majorities; that is, the idolatrous absolutes claimed for any value, person, or institution. By subverting cherished truths, Jews are expected to push the world to see new alternatives, alternative ways to heal the pains and the fears of humanity. Jewish tradition asks its followers to foster human dignity and uniqueness, extend the potential for life and goodness over death and evil. The task is to increase their responsibility as partners with God.

As Moses approaches the end of his life, he speaks of the obligation to pursue the covenantal relationships that are at the core of the Torah and the Jewish story:

It is not too hard for you nor beyond your reach. It is not in the heavens, that you should say: "Who will go up for us to the heavens and bring it down to us, that we may do it?" Nor is it beyond the sea, that you should say: "Who will cross the sea for us and bring it over to us, that we may do it?" No, it is very near to you, in your mouth and in your heart, and you can do it. (Deuteronomy 30:11-14)

11

TOWARD HEALING AND WHOLENESS: ON THE ROAD TO THE MESSIAH

"And you can do it." For those who have struggled with all the questions and fears and finally made the existential choice to renew the ancient covenant between the Jewish people and God and accept the responsibility of repairing the world, the method is clear: *kedushah* is increased in the world through the *mitzvot*, those acts by which we participate in creation and consciously raise the common to the sacred. But anyone who makes a way through this world must eventually face fatigue, grief, doubt, and disappointment. What are the sources in Judaism for solace and renewal? As a young man at a recent lecture I gave demanded to know: "What of healing and wholeness? Where is there a place in Judaism for inadequacy and failure? Who will comfort me when I no longer have the energy or capacity to fight?"

Indeed, failure can overwhelm the best of intentions and the greatest courage. In spite of men and women of good-will, the world remains filled with suffering and violence. Often, there seems so little that anyone can do to help the vulnerable and downtrodden, not to mention heal the pains or assuage the angers of those closest to us. Ultimately, we cannot save even those we love most from death.

Eugene Borowitz writes that our response to just these kinds of failures may be a priority for any religious agenda:

> We did not anticipate the possibility of deep and lasting failure. We could not believe that our best ideas might be too small, our plans inadequate, our character mean, our wills perverse. We certainly did not expect that in doing righteousness, we might also create evil, sometimes ones so great that they seemed to outweigh the good we had done. . . . Knowing our failures, we cannot truly believe in ourselves. We cannot even do the good which lies within our power, because failure has convinced us that nothing we might do is worth anything. If religion could teach secular society to accept failure without becoming paralyzed and to reach for forgiveness without mitigating our sense of responsibility, we might end the dejection and moral lassitude which now suffuses our civilization.[1]

Religious voices can both comfort and empower those who feel themselves abandoned and rudderless. Faith can be a force for meaning and direction. As Harold Schulweis so aptly taught me: "Do not inquire if one believes in God. Challenge a person to discover in what God or gods he or she believes." The question is not simply whether the beliefs are true, but what difference does that faith make in one's life and what are the effects of those beliefs. This has been a century of unusual disillusionment in the gods we pursued.

These are some of the Jewish principles that can heal and comfort in troubled times, as well as ultimately lead us toward the messianic goal:

FAITH IN CREATION

The sages who authored the *Mishnah*, like the Jewish leaders living in the shadow of the Holocaust, had to face a world in which all the signposts of God's presence had evaporated. With no Temple and no Jerusalem, bereft of any evidence of God's love, the postexilic community still found the confidence to believe. They found this faith in the creation itself. In the daily liturgy they authored, the sages looked at the world and saw in it God's sustaining presence. They praised God as the source of light and darkness, of the seasons and the cycles of time. They imagined men and women standing on the edge of the universe as if surveying it for the first time, marveling at its form, harmony, and order.

The implications of this affirmation are profound. Children learn early that there are rules in this world that nurture life, that night is not to be feared for the sun will rise again in the morning. In short, they can believe in the future. Roland Gittelsohn speaks of this faith:

> The creator will continue to move the universe according to the same dependable physical laws by which it was created and through which it has evolved since the beginning of time. It will never rain in the total absence of moisture-laden clouds, never snow when the air temperature is above ninety degrees Fahrenheit. . . . I can depend on all of this; I can make my plans and stake my life on it.[2]

Of course, one can *choose* to see only randomness in the universe and life as a coincidence of carbon, light, and energy. Thus, Carl Sagan and Ann Druyan write:

If the Earth were as old as a person, a typical organism would be born, live and die in a sliver of a second. We are fleeting, transitional creatures, snowflakes fallen on the hearth fire.[3]

This view does not reflect objective truth so much as a deep and subjective alienation. To state that human life is meaningless is an assertion based on faith, exactly as is the assertion that the world was created with conscious order and inherent goodness. Its impact, though, is far more problematic. The physicist Roger Jones notes: "For the first time in history, a culture has conjured up a story about itself that altogether denies any meaning, value or purpose in human existence."[4]

To be a Jew, to have faith in the meaning of creation, allows one to see a universe moving from chaos toward order and empowers scientists to find further evidence of that order. With confidence that they are only revealing that which is already present, physicists and astronomers probe deeper into the skies, finding ripples in the pattern of energy waves that confirm the instantaneous burst of light-energy that formed the universe: "Let there be light," proclaims Genesis, "and there was light" (Genesis 1:3).

Judaism permits a person to posit that his or her existence is part of a thrilling explosion of life forces, ever increasing in richness and wonderful complexity. And so, genes are spliced, DNA molecules replicated, and organs transplanted, paradoxically multiplying the common bonds as well as the intrinsic uniqueness of life:

Embryos, it is widely known, reenact evolutionary history. During our fetal development, we are unicellular. . . . We are fish, we are fowl. And we are primates. We *are* those things.

... This genetic memory seems replete with all our ancestral forms. ... Each person can relive all creation. We can return through our phylogeny back through childhood and parents, mammals, amphibians, and protozoan slime, through volcanoes and cosmic debris to the act of creation itself.[5]

Within each human being is the matter that was present in the moment of creation itself. We breathe the same breath of air as those long gone. And redemption is the completion of creation. "Blessed is God," the sages prompt Jews to say in recognition of this marvelous unfolding, "who renews in goodness each day the primal act of creation." And human beings are meant to consciously witness and participate in this process.

FAITH IN GOD AS A SOURCE OF HOPE

During the months before Rosh HaShanah, when Jews begin to focus on the failures of the past year and the need for *teshuvah* (personal growth and transformation), Psalm 27 is recited twice each day. Ignoring the themes of sin and judgment, the psalmist seeks comfort in God's love:

God is my light and my redemption, then whom should I fear?
God is the strength of my life, then who can frighten me?
Though I am besieged by attackers, my heart is not afraid.
Though battles may beset me, still I am confident.
One thing I ask of God, only this do I desire: that I may live my whole life within God's embrace, to gaze upon the goodness of God, to visit within God's sanctuary.
God will shelter me when I am troubled, protect me in the secrets of God's tent.

Hear me, O Eternal, when I cry out, have mercy and answer me.
Longing after You, my heart calls for God: "Seek My face."
O God, I seek Your face.
Do not hide Your face from me;
Do not abandon me or forsake me, O God, my deliverer.
Though my father and mother abandon me, the Eternal will
embrace me.
Parent me in Your ways.
That I will savor the goodness of God in the land of the living.
(Excerpts from Psalm 27)

The psalmist does not expect anything from God. His words are an expression of his faith that the human struggle has meaning, that life is intrinsically good. His belief in God is a way to express these convictions. His prayer is not an Aladdin's brass lamp to rub and magically receive a wish but an attempt to get closer to God as a source of strength and hope:

Prayer cannot mend a broken bridge, rebuild a ruined city, or bring water to parched fields.
Prayer can mend a broken heart, lift up a discouraged soul, and strengthen a weakened will.[6]

The relationship of prayer is as much with the hidden God as with the God whose gifts are apparent and palpable. The faith in a sustaining Presence in the world can empower an individual and give a community the strength to build and renew.

God is the infinite source from which human beings replenish their energy to change themselves and the world. For, as has been described, Judaism values the process of change as much as change itself. The rabbinic dictum "The reward for doing one *mitzvah* is (doing) another *mitzvah*" serves as a reminder that *kedushah* is not a state of being but incremental movements in a spiraling orbit toward the core of Godliness. Again, Gittelsohn notes:

> I am convinced that within the whole adventure there has been an active agent, an innate thrust toward life, toward ever more complex, sensitive forms of life, finally toward the pursuit of truth, beauty, and goodness. That energy, that thrust is God. I can expect God to endorse change and growth in the future, as God has in the past.[7]

God can be an ever-replenishing source of energy because, the *Midrash* states, unlike ourselves, God does not tire of human failure:

> "Cast your burden upon the Eternal, and God will sustain you (Psalm 55)." A person may have a patron. You ask for help once or twice and are received. The third time the patron pretends to be busy; the fourth time, the patron turns away from you entirely. But God is not like that. Whenever you worry God, God will receive you.[8]

God is present in the lives of human beings even when they feel unworthy:

> A nonbeliever gloats to Rabbi Hanina: "Now that the Temple is destroyed and you cannot cleanse yourselves of all your impurities, God no longer will dwell with you." Rabbi Hanina replied: It is written, "God dwells with you in the midst of all your impurities."[9]

In Judaism, God is manifest in the world not by the word that becomes flesh or by miraculous acts, but through the human desire to improve the self and disseminate life and goodness over death and evil. God is present whenever we dare to hope, even in the face of despair. Vaclav Havel, the Czech playwright/president, exemplified that spirit in the face of persecution when he wrote:

> Hope is an orientation of the spirit, an orientation of the heart. It is not the conviction that something will turn out well, but the certainty that something makes sense, regardless of how it turns out.[10]

Belief in God does not automatically make one happy, but it does provide reasons to continue to struggle against forces that seem overwhelming. The alternative, realistic as it may seem, deadens the spirit and paralyzes the will. Through belief in God's transcendent meaning, a person chooses to believe in life itself. That is why faith can exist even in the darkest settings—because ultimately such affirmation is an expression of hope for life. You hear the echo of Jewish faith from an anonymous inscription found on the wall of a cellar in Cologne, where a Jewish family hid from the Nazis:

> I believe in the sun even when it is not shining.
> I believe in love even when not feeling it.
> I believe in God even when God is silent.

FAITH IN RELATIONSHIP

In the middle of the night, on the path back home to *Eretz Yisrael*, Jacob the patriarch wrestles with an unnamed assailant. Some biblical commentators call his opponent an angel of God, but a far more intriguing interpretation comes from those who imagine the nocturnal attacker to be another dimension of Jacob himself, one that he has tried to suppress. It is not unusual for human beings to project onto others that which they hate in themselves. Alone and frightened,

> It comes back to injure and name us during the night. And since it is still a part of ourselves we cannot bear to acknowledge, when we sense it in someone else, we are all the more frightened and angry. . . . Once we realize that what we detest in another person only wants to be accepted, taken back, and loved, do we begin to diminish our own capacity for evil. . . . We heal and redeem it and, in so doing, we heal ourselves and God.[11]

There can be no redemption without this healing process. Commitment to the covenant means working with others, divine and human. After his struggle with his own dark side, Jacob can live more fully and effectively. He can return to his wives and children, with all the complex feelings and uneasy dynamics of those relationships. He can embrace his brother, Esau, whom he once deceived and feared. He can reunite with his aged and infirm parents, and care for them. Jacob is renewed and renamed Israel, one who has struggled in relationship with a messenger. Having been locked in that struggle all the night, a dawning arrives, and he is victorious. All Jews are the children of Israel.

Judaism recognizes that no person alone can make oneself whole:

> Rabbi Hiyya bar Abba fell ill, and Rabbi Johanan went to visit him. He said to him: "Do you want to suffer so?" Rabbi Hiyya

replied: "Neither the suffering nor any reward for suffering (perhaps a place in heaven)." Rabbi Johanan said to him: "Give me your hand." He gave him his hand, and Rabbi Johanan healed him.

The same Rabbi Johanan once fell ill, and Rabbi Hanina went to visit him. He said to him: "Do you want to suffer so?" He replied, "Neither the suffering nor any reward for suffering." Rabbi Hanina said to him: "Give me your hand." He gave him his hand and Rabbi Hanina healed him.

Why could Rabbi Johanan (who had healed Rabbi Hiyya) not heal himself? The rabbis replied: "The prisoner cannot free himself from jail."[12]

Accepting the love of another and returning it is another way one experiences God's presence. The midrash relates that when the Israelites stood at Sinai, the Torah records that God resided in their midst only when the people looked into each other's eyes (Numbers 14:14). God speaks with them only when they stand "face to face" (Deuteronomy 5:4)—that is, two "images of God" aware of the divinity in each other.

The world is filled with potential others with whom one can create relationship: the family within which one is nurtured, the lover with whom one builds a life, children who are both the products of love and new sources of loving, friends who are soulmates, colleagues with whom one works. Judaism calls on human beings to increase kedushah in their lives and in the world through relationships in which God also can be present. There is no path to the messiah when one seeks and struggles alone. The chasidic sage Rabbi Levi Yitzhak of Berditchev said on this matter: "Whether a person really loves God can be determined by the love that person shares with others." By linking our lives to others, we transcend our finite existence and become closer to God.

Lawrence Kushner speaks of each human lifetime as pieces
of a puzzle, each soul assembling the parts, each in need of
another:

> Everyone carries with them at least one and probably
> Many pieces to someone else's puzzle.
> Sometimes they know it.
> Sometimes they don't.
> And when you present your piece
> Which is worthless to you,
> To another, whether you know it or not,
> Whether they know it or not,
> You are a messenger from the Most High.[13]

FAITH IN REDEMPTION: ON THE PATH OF THE MESSIAH

"The central paradigm of the Jewish religion," writes Irving
Greenberg, "is redemption."[14] While the belief in the divine
image in human beings affirms the value of each human
being, a partnership with God that seeks wholeness and redemption goes beyond the personal. The messianic potential for all humanity enters history through the events of the
Exodus. Greenberg continues:

> Exodus points to a future goal in that it promises that not
> only Jews will reach the Promised Land of freedom and equal-
> ity but all people will. . . . Judaism has built into its own self-
> understanding that it must generate future messianic mo-
> ments. And the central revealed metaphor that guides this
> process from the beginning is covenant . . . [that] makes pos-
> sible the process of getting to the final redemption. The cove-
> nant is Israel's commitment not to stop short of perfection.[15]

The Exodus was nothing less than a transformation of consciousness, announcing that what the world heretofore had accepted as natural or preordained was the result of human inadequacy hardened into absolutes. The Exodus proclaimed that those precedents could be shattered, that absolutes need not be sacred. It called on Jews to subvert complacent realities by imagining a truly just world. That world is not the *mishpat* of the nations or even that of Jewish kings, which Jews are called upon to respect and obey, but the *tzedek* of God, the unknowable absolute. The Torah as well as the historical experience of the Jewish people are the narratives from which the strategy for bringing on redemption can be envisioned. Greenberg explains:

> The messianic dream is the great moving force of Jewish history and of the Jewish role in the world. It is the natural unfolding and universal application of the Exodus experience. The central biblical event—the overthrow of tyranny, the redemption of the Jewish slaves, and the gift of freedom and dignity—will become the experience of all humankind in the future kingdom of God. . . . Setting in motion a subversive discontent, creating an explosive tension between the ideal and the real, Judaism has transformed the world again and again.[16]

There is no shortcut on the messianic path toward a redeemed world other than methodically elevating each moment and event from commonness to *kedushah*, turning human behavior into *mitzvah*. Abraham Joshua Heschel reminds us of the human capacity to be Godlike:

> Judaism is a theology of the common deed, of the trivialities of life, dealing not so much with the training for the

exceptional, as with the management of the trivial. . . . Thus, the purpose seems to be to ennoble the common, to endow worldly things with hieratic beauty; to attune the comparative to the absolute, to associate the detail with the whole, to adapt our own being with its plurality, conflicts and contradictions, to the all-transcending unity, to the holy.[17]

How does a people live with one foot planted in the mundane present and the other in a messianic future? By proceeding one step at a time, as part of an endless chain of human effort. By seeing in each discrete action the possibility for transcendence. By being willing to bear the weight of a world in dire need of healing and by being ready to participate in its perfection even if the changes one can make are too minute to be seen by the human eye.

Lawrence Kushner, a contemporary rabbi, offers a messianic vision of how the *kedushah* emanating from such minute acts can infuse and ultimately transform the world:

> Entrances to holiness are everywhere.
> The possibility of ascent is all the time.
> Even at unlikely times and through places.
> "There is no place on earth without the Presence."
> (*Numbers Rabbah* 12:4)[18]

This expansive holiness is part of the process in which a covenant enforced by contract is replaced by a voluntary covenant, a stage in the messianic unfolding that the prophet Jeremiah foretold: "It will not be like the covenant I made with their ancestors. . . . I will put My teaching into their innermost being and inscribe it upon their hearts. Then I will become their God and they, My people" (Jeremiah 31:33).

Frightening as it may be to depend upon individuals to voluntarily choose to live within the orbit of *kedushah* and commit to repair the world, there is no other direction on the path to the messiah.

That is why Judaism must effect more than a harmony between its traditions and those of Western civilization, as Jews have tried so hard to do in the last century. Judaism must offer a compelling alternative narrative for the Jews of North America, one that is a captivating source of meaning and joy. The contemporary Jewish community must learn to articulate the distinctiveness of its mission and its unique methodology for achieving that ideal. The enticements of American culture that absorb and flatten diversity can be met and overcome through the power of the Jewish story retold. The Jewish narrative of transformation and redemption is its most powerful tool:

> It can come as no surprise that only a people with a narrative can flourish in a hostile society, because only a people with a narrative can engage in affirming cooperation. A people with a narrative identify both with one another and with shared positive goals. Moreover, they take enormous delight in having a hand in the realization of these goals.[19]

Jews must affirm their role as constructive subversives, even as they call on others to join in repairing this world. For it is in *this world* that healing will replace sickness, that poverty and oppression will be overcome, and that human dignity will prove infinite. The complacent acceptance of unjust economic, social, and political systems will be shaken as the systems that upheld them crumble. And life will triumph:

Faith is not a fairy tale. If all this does not happen, then the whole Torah is an illusion, a fable. This affirmation is part of the courage and daring of Judaism. Judaism insists that redemption is going to happen in this world, where you can see it, measure it.[20]

The path is not unilinear and its length is unknown. History often has proved disappointing. Yet Jews must believe that *tikkun olam* is possible. A contemporary rabbinical statement conveys the power of memory and of hope in the Jewish affirmation:

We have lived through terrible tragedy and been compelled to reappropriate our tradition's realism about the human capacity for evil. Yet our people has always refused to despair. The survivors of the Holocaust, on being granted life, seized it, nurtured it and, rising above catastrophe, showed humankind that the spirit is indomitable. The State of Israel, established and maintained by the Jewish will to live, demonstrates what a united people can accomplish in history. The existence of the Jew is an argument against despair; Jewish survival is warrant for human hope.[21]

Being a Jew in this era, as in the prior millennia, means to accept the rabbinical dictum, "You are not obligated to complete the task, but you also are not free to ignore what must be done."[22]

RETELLING THE STORY FOR OUR TIME

Every people tells a story and, in every age, new ways of telling the story must be imagined and cultivated. The purpose of the story is not to describe events, but to nourish a community's commitment to the present and faith in the future. Joseph B. Soloveitchik explains:

> To tell a story is to relive an event. We still sit on the floor and mourn the destruction of the sanctuary, an event which took place 1,900 years ago. We still celebrate the Exodus, an event which lies in the dawn of our history. Our stories are concerned not only with the past, but with the future as well. We tell our children the story of . . . waiting for the great realization of the promise, no matter how slow the realization is in coming. . . . Our story unites countless generations; present, past, and future merge into one great experience.[23]

The stories of Eastern Europe, of *bubbes* and *zaydies* and flickering Sabbath candles illuminating the freezing landscape outside *shtetl* homes in Russia, must now make space for the suffering and survival of the Holocaust, the drama of establishing and building an independent Jewish state, and the hopes of a flourishing Jewish community breathing democracy and freedom in North America. The new stories are intimate and personal, grand and sweeping. They will speak in the idioms of life at the dawn of the twenty-first century, of the experiences of a generation born into a transformed world. But the search for meaning remains as intense and critical today as it was for Abraham and Sarah.

I return to my own tale, which has been and creates expressions of meaning in my life. My mother, as a teenager, managed to escape to England shortly after Kristallnacht, the 1938 pogrom of shattered glass. Her parents and sister soon followed. All the papers had been processed to bring out my great-grandmother, but the war broke out first—and the iron grip of the Nazis closed on her. She and the rest of my family were trapped in Germany.

My grandmother, Mutti, never knew when and where her mother died, so she recited the memorial *kaddish* prayer each year on her mother's birthday. The family only knew that she had last been seen alive in Theresienstadt, a Nazi concentration camp near Prague. In 1990, my family traveled to Prague as part of a pilgrimage to the Europe of our past and the Israel of our miraculous present. I had visited Mutti several weeks before we left for Europe and promised to research the archives at the Theresienstadt camp for any information about her mother.

The maniacal deliberateness of the Nazis provided volumes of data: transports loaded with human cargo, into the camp for deposit, out of the camp to death. I moved through the German records and, within minutes, lifted my great-grandmother's name from the Nazi oblivion, locating the transport on which she had arrived at the camp and the train that later dragged her to a pit in Poland, where she was murdered.

I called Mutti from Europe with the news that the long wait was over; her mother's murder was resolved. But she did not live to recite *kaddish* for her mother on the anniversary of that murder. Mutti died two weeks later, shortly before her ninety-third birthday, on the day we returned from Israel to see her and tell her the story. The following month was Yom Kippur, the most sacred day of the Jewish calendar. Our family lit a candle of memory and recited the *kaddish* for both mother and daughter, for it was on the Day of Atonement, 1942, that my great-grandmother had been murdered.

One very old Jewish tradition predicts that the messiah will arrive on the Day of Atonement, the Sabbath of Sabbaths.

Our first child, Talia, was born on Yom Kippur, 1976, a new partner in the generations that walk the path toward redemption. Her story, along with Noam, Yaron, Liore, and others of their generation, awaits the new meanings that Jews steeped in an awareness of the past and the possibilities of the future will give it.

A long time ago, another story was told which nurtured a family, molded a people, and offered hope to humanity. Abraham and Sarah were promised that their progeny would be a great people in their own land and that all the families of the earth would be blessed through them. Their children told and retold that story on their long odyssey, a history of passionate commitment, obstinacy, faithlessness, love, and ultimate perseverance. They told the story by reenacting it and reinterpreting it. The promise to Abraham and Sarah led to the covenant at Sinai and the foundation in *Eretz Yisrael* of a unique society seeking greater *kedushah*. With exile, the promise expanded to encompass every aspect of being, like perfume released from its container.

For the first time in history, at the dawn of the twenty-first century, the Jewish people has the potential to fulfill all aspects of the biblical promise made to Abraham and Sarah: A strong Jewish state in *Eretz Yisrael* can be a model of rebirth, as a vibrant, change-oriented Jewish community throughout the world can serve as a blessing. The renewal of the Jewish mission requires that Jews immerse themselves in their own civilization and create additional authentic ways of retelling their remarkable story. The initial task is to rebuild lost connections by exploring with care the Jewish experiences and expressions of the past—ideas, rituals, language, visions, texts, and celebrations, a veritable treasure of meaning and direction for each human being, for families and communities, and for the world—and to determine what to hold sacred. Out of this encounter with Jewish traditions will grow commitment and love, no less for this generation than it did for Jews of the past. And out of commitment and love will emerge the passionate desire and will to find ways to fulfill the Jewish mission: to subvert the present in an effort to achieve the unimaginable.

NOTES

INTRODUCTION

1. Harold Kushner, *When All You've Ever Wanted Isn't Enough* (New York: Summit Books, 1965), p. 18.

2. *Musaf* liturgy, Rosh HaShanah.

3. Harold Schulweis, "High Holiday message," unpublished, 1977.

4. David G. Roskies, *Against the Apocalypse* (Cambridge, MA: Harvard University Press, 1984), p. 20.

CHAPTER 1

1. *Zohar: The Book of Enlightenment*, trans. Daniel Chanan Matt (New York: Paulist Press, 1983), pp. 44–45.

2. *Pirkei Avot* 3:18.

3. Carl Sagan and Ann Druyan, *Shadows of Forgotten Ancestors* (New York: Random House, 1992), p. 99.

4. See Jon Levenson, *Creation and the Persistence of Evil* (San Francisco: Harper & Row, 1969).

5. Sagan and Druyan, *Shadows of Forgotten Ancestors*, p. 80.

6. Jean-Paul Sartre, *Nausea*, trans. Lloyd Alexander (New York: New Directions, 1964), p. 39.

7. *Mishnah Sanhedrin* 4:5.

8. Ibid.

9. Ibid.

10. Ibid.

11. Irwin Kula, "Seeking a Sense of Mitzvah," *Sh'ma* 24:466 (January 1944): 1.

Chapter 2

1. Babylonian Talmud, *Niddah* 16a.

2. Michael Wyschograd, *The Body of Faith* (Minneapolis: Seabury Press, 1983), pp. 91–92.

3. David Biale, *Eros and Judaism* (New York: Basic Books, 1992), p. 15.

4. Ibid., p. 31.

Chapter 3

1. From the *Haggadah* of Passover.

2. J. P. M. Walsh, *The Mighty from Their Thrones* (Philadelphia: Fortress Press, 1987), p. 21.

3. CTA 5.2.5–6, cited in Walsh, *The Mighty from Their Thrones*, p. 21.

4. CTA 5.6.23–24, cited in Walsh, *The Mighty from Their Thrones* p. 21.

5. CTA 6.6.47–48, cited in Walsh, *The Mighty from Their Thrones*, p. 21.

6. Michael Lerner, *Jewish Renewal: A Path to Healing and Transformation* (New York: G. P. Putnam's Sons, 1994), p. 127.

Chapter 4

1. Jon D. Levenson, *Sinai and Zion* (New York: Harper & Row, 1987), p. 86.

2. Babylonian Talmud, *Shabbat* 88a.

3. W. Gunther Plaut, *The Torah, A Modern Commentary* (New York: Union of American Hebrew Congregations, 1981), p. 517.

4. Babylonian Talmud, *Berakhot* 8b.

5. David Hartman, *A Living Covenant* (New York: Free Press, 1985), p. 262.

6. Ibid.

7. Michael Wyschograd, *The Body of Faith* (Minneapolis: Winston Press, 1983), p. 17.

8. For an analysis of the three eras of the Jewish people, see Irving Greenberg's *The Third Great Cycle of Jewish History* (New York: National Jewish Center for Learning and Leadership, 1981).

9. Michael Lerner, *Jewish Renewal: A Path to Healing and Transformation* (New York: G. P. Putnam's Sons, 1994), p. 121.

10. Josephus Flavius, *The Jewish Wars*, trans. William Whinton (Grand Rapids, MI: Kregel Publications, 1981), p. 561.

CHAPTER 5

1. Jon D. Levenson, *Sinai and Zion* (New York: Harper & Row, 1987), p. 42.

2. *Mekhilta* 42b and the Babylonian Talmud, *Gittin* 56b.

3. *Avot D'Rabbi Natan* 4:21.

4. Lawrence Fine, *Safed Spirituality* (New York: Paulist Press, 1984), pp. 65-67.

5. Rabbi Nahman,"*Likutay Moharan*," in *Tikkun* (Jerusalem: Breslov Research Institute, 1984), chap. 1.

6. Salo W. Baron, "Population," in *Encyclopaedia Judaica* (Jerusalem: Keter Publishing House, 1971), pp. 878-882.

CHAPTER 7

1. Arthur Hertzberg, *The French Enlightenment and the Jews* (New York: Columbia University Press, 1968), p. 360.

2. Ibid. p. 368.

3. Samson Raphael Hirsch, "Religion in Union with Progress," in *Judaism Eternal*, ed. and trans. I. Grunfeld, vol. 2 (London: Sonomo, 1956), pp. 224-238.

4. Excerpt, translation by Shira Milgrom.

5. Paul Mendes-Flohr and Jehuda Reinharz, *The Jew in the Modern World* (New York: Oxford University Press, 1980), p. 118.

6. Ismar Schorsch, *Jewish Responses to German Anti-Semitism* (New York: Columbia University Press, 1972), p. 57.

7. *Yearbook*, vol. 45 (New York: Central Conference of American Rabbis, 1935), pp. 198-200.

8. Schorsch, *Jewish Responses to German Anti-Semitism*, p. 57.

9. Letter of 6 May 1926, in Ernst L. Freud, ed., *Letters of Sigmund Freud* (New York: 1961), p. 220.

10. *Sifrei Deuteronomy*, Piska 22.

11. Schorsch, *Jewish Reponses to German Anti-Semitism*, p. 49.

12. For a more thorough analysis of the ethics of power and power-lessness, see Irving Greenberg's article in *The Ethics of Jewish Power: Two Views* (New York: Jewish Center for Learning and Leadership, 1987).

13. See Irving Greenberg, *Auschwitz: Beginning of a New Era* (New York: Jewish Center for Learning and Leadership; reprint, 1975).

14. Primo Levi, *Survival at Auschwitz* (New York: Collier Books, 1958), p. 135.

15. Ibid., p. 118.

16. Greenberg, *Auschwitz*.

17. George Orwell, *1984* (New York: New American Library, 1949), pp. 210-211.

18. Levi, *Survival at Auschwitz*, p. 8.

19. Irving Greenberg, *Voluntary Covenant* (New York: National Jewish Center for Learning and Leadership, 1982), p. 35.

20. Chaim Weizman, "Testimony Before the Anglo-American Commission," cited in *Jewish Wisdom*, ed. Joseph Telushkin (New York: William Morrow, 1994), pp. 655-656.

21. Irwin Kula, "Seeking a Sense of Mitzvah," *Sh'ma* 24:466 (January 1994): 4.

22. For a further development of the principles of a post-Holocaust voluntary covenant for the Jewish people and of its affirmation of life, see Greenberg, *Voluntary Covenant*.

CHAPTER 8

1. I am indebted to my in-laws, Drs. Jo and Jacob Milgrom, whose insights and teaching have illumined my understanding of *kedushah* and *mitzvah*.

2. Martin Buber, *Ten Rungs: Hassidic Sayings* (New York: Schocken Books, 1947), p. 5.

3. Pablo Casals, *Joys and Sorrows* (New York: Simon & Schuster, 1974), p. 17.

4. Babylonian Talmud, *Berakhot* 35a.

5. Benediction from the Daily Prayer Book.

6. Babylonian Talmud, *Kiddushin* 31a.

7. Abraham Joshua Heschel, *Who Is Man?* (Stanford, CA: Stanford University Press, 1965), p. 111.

CHAPTER 9

1. Abraham Joshua Heschel, *The Insecurity of Freedom* (New York: Schocken Books, 1972), p. 68.

2. W. Gunther Plaut, *The Torah, A Modern Commentary* (New York: Union of American Hebrew Congregations, 1981), p. 992.

3. Babylonian Talmud, *Sanhedrin* 27b.

4. *Avot d'Rabbi Natan*, verse I, VII, 17a.

5. *Sifre* Deuteronomy 49.

6. Maimonides, *Mishneh Torah*, Gifts to the Needy 10:1-2.

7. Maimonides, *Mishneh Torah*, Gifts to the Needy 7:1-3.

8. Lawrence Fine, *Safed Spirituality* (New York: Paulist Press, 1984), p. 37.

9. Yosef Karo, *Shulhan Arukh, Yoreh De'ah* 251:3.

10. Reuven Kimelman, *Tsedakah and Us* (New York: National Jewish Center for Learning and Leadership, 1983), p. 17.

11. Babylonian Talmud, *Gittin* 61a.

12. Maimonides, *Mishneh Torah*, *Avodat Kohavim*, 10:5.

13. Babylonian Talmud, *Ketubot* 68a.

14. J. P. M. Walsh, *The Mighty from Their Thrones* (Philadelphia: Fortress Press, 1987), p. 4.

15. Ibid., p. 5.

16. Maimonides, *Mishneh Torah*, Gifts to the Needy 10:1-2.

17. Walsh, *The Mighty from Their Thrones*, p. 63.

18. *Itturei Torah, Parashat Zakhor* (Tel Aviv: Yavneh, 1990).

Chapter 10

1. James Q. Wilson, *The Moral Sense* (New York: The Free Press, 1993), p. xii.

2. Marshall Berman, *All That Is Solid Melts into Air* (New York: Penguin Books, 1988), p. 21.

3. Kenneth Gergen, *The Saturated Self* (New York: Basic Books, 1991), p. 85.

4. Joseph Telushkin, *Jewish Humor* (New York: William Morrow, 1992), p. 27.

5. Philip Roth, *Portnoy's Complaint* (New York: Bantam Books, 1970), p. 134.

6. Harold Schulweis, "Empowering the Jewish Family," unpublished sermon, 1977.

7. Peter Berger, *The Homeless Minds*, cited in Kenneth J. Gergen, *The Saturated Self* (New York: Basic Books, 1991), p. 73.

8. Irwin Kula, "Seeking a Sense of Mitzvah," *Sh'ma* 24:466 (January 1994): 3.

9. Robert Cole, *The Call of Stories* (Boston: Houghton Mifflin, 1989), p. 30.

10. Babylonian Talmud, *Sotah* 14a.

11. Leonard Fein, "Smashing Idols and Other Prescriptions for Jewish Continuity" (New York: Nathan Cummings Foundation, 1994), p. 42.

12. Mishnah *Semahot*, chap. 1.

13. *Sefer Hasidim* 793.

14. Immanuel Jakobovitz, *Jewish Medical Ethics* (New York: Bloch, 1975), p. 124.

15. *Pirkei Avot* 5:18.

16. *Avot D'Rabbi Natan* 8.

17. Sara Bershtal, *Saving Remnants: Feeling Jewish in America* (New York: Free Press, 1992), pp. 283-284.

18. "Making Love as Making Justice: Towards a New Jewish Ethic of Sexuality," a paper presented at the American Academy of Religion, Kansas City, MO, Nov. 24, 1991, p. 6.

19. Mark Johnson, *Moral Imagination* (Chicago: University of Chicago Press, 1993), p. 260.

20. Alasdair MacIntyre, *After Virtue*, 2nd ed. (Notre Dame, IN: University of Notre Dame Press, 1984), p. 216.

Chapter 11

1. Eugene Borowitz, "Religious Values in a Secular Society," *Journal of Ecumenical Studies* 21:3 (Summer 1984): 544.

2. Roland B. Gittelsohn, "Why I Am a Religious Naturalist," in *Reform Judaism* (New York: Central Conference of American Rabbis, 1991), pp. 22-23.

3. Carl Sagan and Ann Druyan, *Shadows of Forgotten Ancestors* (New York: Random House, 1992), p. 31.

4. Roger Jones, *Physics for the Rest of Us* (Chicago: Contemporary Books, 1992), p. 133.

5. Lawrence Kushner, *River of Light* (Chappaqua, NY: Rossel Books, 1981), p. 85.

6. Ferdinand M. Isserman, cited in *Entrances to Holiness Are Everywhere*, prayer book (White Plains, NY: Jewish Community Center, 1993), p. 22b.

7. Gittelsohn, "Why I Am a Religious Naturalist," p. 22.

8. *Midrash* on Psalm 55:22.

9. Babylonian Talmud, *Yoma* 56b-57a.

10. Vaclav Havel, cited in *Entrances to Holiness Are Everywhere*, p. 52b.

11. Lawrence Kushner, *God Was in This Place and I, i Did Not Know* (Woodstock, VT: Jewish Lights, 1991), p. 70.

12. Babylonian Talmud, *Berakhot* 5b.

13. Lawrence Kushner, *Honey from the Rock* (Woodstock, VT: Jewish Lights, 1990), p. 70.

14. Irving Greenberg, *The Jewish Way* (New York: Summit Books, 1988), p. 18.

15. Irving Greenberg, "The Relationship of Judaism and Christianity: Toward a New Organic Model," *Quarterly Review* 4 (Winter 1984): 5.

16. Greenberg, *The Jewish Way*, p. 19.

17. Abraham Joshua Heschel, *Man Is Not Alone: A Philosophy of Religion* (New York: Harper & Row, 1951), p. 271.

18. Kushner, *Honey from the Rock*, p. 48.

19. Lawrence Thomas, *Vessels of Evil: American Slavery and the Holocaust* (Philadelphia: Temple University Press, 1993).

20. Irving Greenberg, "The Relationship of Judaism and Christianity: Toward a New Organic Model," *Quarterly Review* 4 (Winter 1984): 5.

21. "Centenary Perspective," *Yearbook,* vol. 86 (New York: Central Conference of American Rabbis, 1976), p. 175.

22. *Pirkei Avot* 2:15.

23. Joseph B. Soloveitchik, "The Community," *Tradition: A Journal of Jewish Responsibility* (Winter 1978): 11.

BIBLIOGRAPHY

Baron, Salo W. "Population." In *Encyclopaedia Judaica*. Jerusalem: Keter Publishing House, 1971.

Bellah, George A., et al. *Postmodern Theology*. San Francisco: Harper, 1989.

Berger, Peter. *The Homeless Minds*. Cited in Kenneth J. Gergen, *The Saturated Self*. New York: Basic Books, 1991.

Berger, Peter L. *The Social Construction of Reality*. New York: Anchor Books, 1969.

Berkovits, Eliezer. *Not in Heaven*. New York: KTAV Publishing, 1983.

Berman, Marshall. *All That Is Solid Melts into Air*. New York: Penguin Books, 1988.

Bershtal, Sara. *Saving Remnants: Feeling Jewish in America*. New York: Free Press, 1992.

Biale, David. *Eros and Judaism*. New York: Basic Books, 1992.

Borowitz, Eugene. "Religious Values in a Secular Society." *Journal of Ecumenical Studies* 21:3 (Summer 1984): 544.

Buber, Martin. *Ten Rungs: Hassidic Savings*. New York: Schocken Books, 1947.

Casals, Pablo. *Joys and Sorrows*. New York: Simon & Schuster, 1974.

Cohen, Steven M. *American Assimilation or Jewish Revival?* Indianapolis: Indiana University Press, 1988.

Cole, Robert. *The Call of Stories*. Boston: Houghton Mifflin, 1989.

Elazar, Daniel J. *Kinship and Consent*. Lanham, MD: University Press of America, 1983.

Eliade, Mircea. *Symbolism, the Sacred, and the Arts.* New York: Continuum, 1992.

Fein, Leonard. "Smashing Idols and Other Prescriptions for Jewish Continuity." New York: The Nathan Cummings Foundation, 1994.

Fine, Lawrence. *Safed Spirituality.* New York: Paulist Press, 1984.

Flavius, Josephus. *The Jewish Wars.* Grand Rapids, MI: Kregel Publications, 1981.

Gergen, Kenneth J. *The Saturated Self.* New York: Basic Books, 1991.

Greenberg, Irving. *The Jewish Way.* New York: Summit Books, 1988.

——. "The Relationship of Judaism and Christianity: Toward a New Organic Model." *Quarterly Review* 4 (Winter 1984): 5.

——. *Voluntary Covenant.* New York: National Jewish Center for Learning and Leadership, 1982.

Hartman, David. *A Living Covenant.* New York: Free Press, 1985.

Hertzberg, Arthur. *The French Enlightenment and the Jews.* New York: Columbia University Press, 1968.

Heschel, Abraham Joshua. *The Insecurity of Freedom.* New York: Schocken Books, 1972.

——. *Man Is Not Alone: A Philosophy of Religion.* New York: Harper & Row, 1951.

——. *Who Is Man?* Stanford, CA: Stanford University Press, 1965.

Hirsch, Samson Raphael. "Religion in Union with Progress." In *Judaism Eternal*, vol. 2. Ed. and trans. I. Grunfeld. London: Sonomo, 1956.

Johnson, Mark. *Moral Imagination.* Chicago: University of Chicago Press, 1993.

Jones, Roger. *Physics for the Rest of Us.* Chicago: Contemporary Books, 1992.

Kimelman, Reuven. *Tsedakah and Us.* New York: National Jewish Center for Learning and Leadership, 1983.

Kula, Irwin. "Seeking a Sense of Mitzvah." *Sh'ma* 24:466 (January 1994): 1.

Kung, Hans. *Theology for the Third Millennium.* New York: Doubleday, 1988.

Kung, Hans, and Tracy, David. *Paradigm Change in Theology.* New York: Crossroad Publishing, 1989.

Kushner, Lawrence. *God Was in This Place and I, i Did Not Know.* Woodstock, VT: Jewish Lights, 1991.

——. *Honey from the Rock.* Woodstock, VT: Jewish Lights, 1990.

———. *River of Light*. Chappaqua, NY: Rossel Books, 1981.

Lakoff, George, and Johnson, Mark. *Metaphors We Live By*. Chicago: University of Chicago Press, 1980.

Lerner, Michael. *Jewish Renewal: A Path to Healing and Transformation*. New York: G.P. Putnam's Sons, 1994.

Levenson, Jon D. *Sinai and Zion*. New York: Harper & Row, 1987.

Levi, Primo. *Survival at Auschwitz*. New York: Collier Books, 1958.

MacIntyre, Alasdair. *After Virtue*, 2nd ed. Notre Dame, IN: University of Notre Dame Press, 1984.

Matt, Daniel Chanan, trans. *Zohar: The Book of Enlightenment*. New York: Paulist Press, 1983.

May, Rollo. *The Cry for Myth*. New York: Dell Publishing, 1991.

Nahman, Rabbi. "Likutay Moharan." In *Tikkun*. Jerusalem: Breslov Research Institute, 1984.

Orwell, George. *1984*. New York: New American Library, 1949.

Plaut, W. Gunther. *The Torah, A Modern Commentary*. New York: Union of American Hebrew Congregations, 1981.

Roskies, David G. *Against the Apocalypse*. Cambridge: Harvard University Press, 1984.

Roth, Philip. *Portnoy's Complaint*. New York: Bantam Books, 1970.

Sagan, Carl, and Druyan, Ann. *Shadows of Forgotten Ancestors*. New York: Random House, 1992.

Sartre, Jean-Paul. *Nausea*. Trans. Lloyd Alexander. New York: New Directions, 1964.

Schorsch, Ismar. *Jewish Responses to German Anti-Semitism*. New York: Columbia University Press, 1972.

Shils, Edward. *Tradition*. Chicago: University of Chicago Press, 1981.

Soloveitchik, Joseph B. "The Community." *Tradition: A Journal of Jewish Responsibility* (Winter 1978): 11.

Telushkin, Joseph. *Jewish Humor*. New York: William Morrow, 1992.

———. *Jewish Wisdom*. New York: William Morrow, 1994.

Thomas, Lawrence. *Vessels of Evil: American Slavery and the Holocaust*. Philadelphia: Temple University Press, 1993.

Walsh, J. P. M. *The Mighty from Their Thrones*. Philadelphia: Fortress Press, 1987.

Yerushalmi, Yosef Hayim. *Zakkor: Jewish History and Jewish Memory*. Seattle: University of Washington Press, 1982.

INDEX

About the Author

David Elcott is the academic vice president of CLAL—The National Jewish Center for Learning and Leadership, developing programs for and teaching in over one hundred communities across North America. He is a lecturer in modern Jewish culture and social transformation and has a doctorate from Columbia University. A nationally known speaker on Jewish history and its implications for Jewish education, policies, and community life, Dr. Elcott has dedicated his career to Jewish continuity in a pluralistic, democratic society. He lives in New York City with his wife, Shira, and their four children.